Confidence of Your Obedience

Favorite Sermon on the Mount Passages

Onesimus Bible Study Series

CYPRESS

Published by Cypress Publications

Copyright © 2025 by Cypress Publications

Manufactured in the United States of America

Cataloging-in-Publication Data

Confidence of your obedience: favorite Sermon on the Mount passages/

Onesimus Bible Study Series

p. cm.

Includes scripture index.

ISBN 979-8-89733-011-9 (pbk.); 979-8-89733-012-6 (ebook)

1. Sermon on the Mount—Criticism, interpretation, etc. 2. Bible. Matthew V-VII. 3. Christian life—Study and teaching. I. Title. II Series.

226.906—dc20

Cover design by Brad McKinnon and Brittany Vander Maas.

For information:

Cypress Publications
3625 Helton Drive,
PO Box HCU,
Florence, AL 35630

www.hcu.edu

Onesimus Bible Study Series

The Onesimus Bible Study Series offers biblical lessons for personal or group study from alumni of International Bible College / Heritage Christian University. Each lesson flows from confidence in Scripture as God's inspired, living, and powerful word. Each respects the ongoing relevance of the Bible as it shows us God's heart and guides our service in the name of Jesus. Every lesson is designed to build faith and encourage Christian living.

Why the name Onesimus? We love the brief book of Philemon, in which Onesimus shines as a stunning example of trusting God more than self or circumstance. The runaway slave met the apostle Paul and encountered God's truth. Out of respect for God—and with Paul's blessing and support—Onesimus chose to return to his owner. He did right by obeying the unfortunate and challenging law of the day despite potentially heavy costs and consequences.

Many of our alumni write beautifully. They also exhibit the servant's heart modeled by Onesimus. Their loyalty to God and submission to Scripture model the faithful excellence of Onesimus. We're blessed to know and serve with such fine brethren. We believe they will bless you too.

Editors of Heritage Christian University Press

CONTENTS

MATTHEW 5:1–16
FRANK C. SCHIPANI

FOCUS PASSAGE
Matthew 5:1–16

INTRODUCTION
Our Lord begins the Sermon on the Mount with what are called the Beatitudes. These are eight character traits or attitudes. These Beatitudes are characteristics of the Kingdom citizens, "servants of the king."[i] Our Lord follows each with a blessing. The term Beatitude originates from the Latin word "beatus," meaning happy or blessed. Our Lord ends this section by exhorting listeners to be salt and light in the world, living out these characteristics in their lives.

GOING DEEPER
The Greek word used by our Lord in this text is μάκαριος (makarios), which refers to a state of being blessed, happy, or

being a "privileged recipient of divine favor."[ii] "Those who are blessed "are the deeply or supremely happy."[iii] True happiness comes from knowing God, serving Him, and growing in faith and godly character. Our Lord goes on to tell us how to be blessed or happy by giving us the following eight Beatitudes.

Poor in Spirit

The poor in spirit can be described as those who "acknowledge our spiritual poverty, indeed our spiritual bankruptcy, before God."[iv]   We do not enter God's Kingdom because of our goodness or through our own perfection. We enter His kingdom by His grace, through our faith, at the time of our baptism. We are utterly dependent on Him. Our Lord told a parable of two men, a Pharisee and a tax collector, who went to the temple to pray. The Pharisee thanked God that he was a righteous man, not like the tax collector. The tax collector would not even look up but beat his chest and said, "God have mercy on me, a sinner" (Luke 19:9–14 CSB). The person who is poor in Spirit is not proud of their own righteousness; they are humbled that God has made them righteous through the blood of Christ. Paul wrote, "For you are saved by grace through faith, and this is not from yourselves; it is God's gift—not from works, so that no one can boast" (Ephesians 2:8–9).

Mourn

Many commentators view this type of mourning as sorrow for our sins and the sins of society. Craig Blomberg writes, "Mourning includes grief caused by both personal sin and loss and social evil and oppression."[v] As we grow in Christ, it is easy to become frustrated with sins that we struggle with. It may feel that we go to God over and over again, asking His forgiveness for the same sins. But that godly sorrow leads to repentance (2 Corinthians 7:10). Repentance is the turning away from our sins. It is in that sorrow that I pray and strategize on how to overcome my personal weaknesses so that I can be a better follower of my Lord. We also mourn over the sin and evil in the world. While we may feel helpless to turn back the wickedness of the world, we can make an impact in our small sphere of influence. As we grow in our faithfulness to Christ and help those around us grow, we can begin to reverse the condition of the world, in a small way, by growing in godliness and helping others grow.

The Meek

The meek are those who have a "humble, gentle attitude."[vi] Rather than being self-centered, the meek place God's will and the needs of others above their own selfish interests. Paul says to "Do nothing out of selfish ambition or conceit, but in humility consider others as more important than yourselves" (Philippians 2:3). Rather than weakness, meekness is having the strength and self-control to place God's will ahead of our own.

Merciful

God's mercy towards us is connected in scripture with our mercy to others. God models mercy and compassion to us and expects us to show that mercy and compassion to others. I can't help but think of the parable of the unmerciful servant in Matthew 18:21–35. In the parable, our Lord related the story of a servant who was forgiven by the king a debt which would have been impossible to repay. The servant sees another servant who owes him money and demands that he repay it. When he is unable to repay the debt, the first servant has his debtor thrown into prison. The king hears of his lack of mercy and throws the first servant into prison. When I struggle with unforgiveness, I remember my terrible sin debt that God has forgiven. When I struggle to show compassion to my fellow person, I am reminded of the compassion that He has for me and for every other human being.

Hunger and Thirst for Righteousness

Just as we mourn our sin and the sins of the world, we long for personal righteousness as for justice in society.[vii] We have a deep longing for God's righteousness in our own actions and in those of society around us. Unlike our sinful desires, which never satisfy us, God will satisfy the one who hungers and thirsts for righteousness.

Pure in Heart

The Word of God tells us to "Keep your heart with all vigilance, for from it flow the springs of life" (Proverbs 4:23 ESV). The source of a spring is the aquifer. That water can become contaminated when pollutants seep through the ground into the water. So it is with our heart. We are surrounded by moral impurity. Television, the internet, movies, music, and other media expose us to profanity, sexuality, and violence. But Paul instructs us to focus on that which is pure (Philippians 4:8). We should seek to stay away from that which would corrupt that purity and focus on that which is good. We should pray for His strength to keep ourselves pure (Psalm 51:10), read His Word (Psalm 119:9), and surround ourselves with Christian brothers and sisters who will provide godly examples, encouragement, and accountability.

Peacemakers

As His children, we are God's representatives (ambassadors, 2 Corinthians 5:20), calling people to be reconciled with God and thus showing them the way to become His children. Our society is divided by ideology, politics, and faith, among other things. Often, we see people vilifying those with whom they disagree. But as Christ's followers, we must be different. We need to be peacemakers. We should not only attempt to reconcile with each other, but ultimately work to reconcile others to God through Christ. May our words, actions, and attitudes not cause division but edify others (Ephesians 4:29).

Persecuted

It's easy for us to think that when we are criticized or shunned by those in society for following Jesus, we are doing something wrong. But Christians throughout history have been persecuted. The apostles all faced persecution, and most died as martyrs, according to tradition. Christians throughout history have faced ridicule, abuse, imprisonment, and even death for following Christ. We should not be surprised that we might face persecution as well. Our Lord told His disciples, "If the world hates you, understand that it hated me before it hated you" (John 15:18).

APPLICATION

The qualities our Lord listed in the prior verses are hardly ones our world would consider as those exhibited by those who are blessed. Our society looks at happiness as financial or career success, good health, material possessions, or doing what makes us happy. This has even crept into churches. The prosperity gospel preachers teach that God blesses a person through health and material blessings. But our Lord's teaching on who is blessed or happy runs contrary to the world's view. Blessing or happiness in the kingdom is not circumstantial, but it is connected to one's faithfulness to God and to His will. Many of those listed as blessed are not those whom society would see as blessed. True happiness is not found in the fading riches or pleasures of this world, but in receiving God's grace and allowing ourselves to be transformed as citizens of the kingdom by demonstrating the attributes of kingdom people.

Our Lord ends this section instructing us to be light in the world. Sometimes we feel that it is hard to be a light for God in a world so full of darkness. But it is in darkness that our lights shine more brightly! In August 2003, the Great Lakes area experienced a regional blackout, with 55 million people losing power. The Metropolitan Detroit area, where I live, was at the edge of the affected area. I remember that on the first night of the blackout, I drove to a neighboring county that had not lost power. As I drove through the darkness, I could see the lights of the city of Brighton from several miles away. Where light is present, darkness must retreat! As Christians, we are reflections of the True Light—whom the darkness cannot overcome (John 1:5, 9).

CONCLUSION

As a Christian who loves the Lord and wants to grow each day in his faith, I see our Lord's instructions in this passage as a path to becoming the person He wants me to become. As I work on these godly attitudes, I not only draw closer to that goal, but I also become an example (salt and light) to others. I pray that I can become the kingdom citizen our Lord describes in this passage and that my attitudes and works will draw others to know, love, and serve Him.

DISCUSSION QUESTIONS

1. Which Beatitude do you resonate with the most? Which one do you struggle with the most?
2. Which Beatitude(s) do you think run most contrary to society's values?
3. What do you think most inhibits us from being lights in this world? What can we do as Christians to better be lights in our world?
4. Think of a time when a non-Christian saw the light of Christ in your attitude or behavior. How did they see Christ in you?

ENDNOTES

[i] Weber, Stuart K., *Matthew*, Holman New Testament Commentary (Nashville: Broadman & Holman, 2000), 57.

[ii] Arndt, William et al., *A Greek-English Lexicon of the New Testament and Other Early Christian Literature* (Chicago: University of Chicago Press, 2000), 611.

[iii] Hanger, Donald A., *Matthew 1-13*. Word Biblical Commentary. (Grand Rapids: Zondervan, 2000), 91.

[iv] Stott, John R. W., *The Message of the Sermon on the Mount (Matthew 5-7): Christian Counter-Culture*, The Bible Speaks Today (Downers Grove: InterVarsity Press, 1985), 39.

[v] Blomberg, Craig. *Matthew*. The New American Commentary, 22, (Nashville: B&H 1992), 98.

[vi] Richards, Lawrence O., *New International Encyclopedia of Bible Words: Based on the NIV and the NASB* (Grand Rapids: Zondervan, 1999), 439.

[vii] Carson, D. A., "Matthew," Page 134 in *The Expositor's Bible Commentary: Matthew, Mark, Luke*, ed. Frank E. Gaebelein (Grand Rapids: Zondervan, 1984), 134.

What To Do With
the Old Testament?
Matthew 5:17–20

Cory Waddell

Focus Passage

Matthew 5:17–20

One Main Thing

Jesus is the lens through which Christians are to interpret and apply the Old Testament scriptures. This means having concern for both the spirit and the letter of the law as we study God's divine code.

Introduction

What is better to abide by: the spirit or the letter of the law? This question makes for some interesting (and often spirited) discussion. It is the challenge of judges and lawmakers to know where they stand as they pursue the rule of law in a country. In spiritual circles, readers of scripture must decide how literally to take the words of the Bible and at what points God is more interested in the overall principle ethics than the literal phrasing.

Historically, this general concept has played a role in Christians determining what to do with the Old Testament in the New Testament era. Are we supposed to do everything written in it? Are we supposed to reject it completely, save for general stories of ethical behavior, because we "are not under law but under grace"?[1] Or is there a more nuanced approach to the Old Testament we must adopt?

In Matthew 5:17–20, Jesus gives listeners to His Sermon on the Mount some critical insight into how His followers should understand and use the Mosaic scriptures. The text sheds light on a couple of key elements: 1) Jesus's own relationship to the law and 2) the enduring authority of scripture. Based on these discussions, listeners are then able to understand what our attitude should be towards the scriptures, what we now call the Old Testament.

Going Deeper

As we prepare to go deeper into this text, it is appropriate to briefly address the contextual setup of the passage. The first twenty verses of Matthew 5 are introductory in nature. In simple terms, we might call the Beatitudes, in verses 1–12, the initial attention getter of the sermon. In verses 13–16, Jesus gives the fundamental reasons for righteous living that flow from the blessings in the Beatitudes. He does this with two simple illustrations of *salt* & *light*. While it is tempting to pull a lot out of these pictures, the basic message is not difficult to ascertain. Salt provides flavor and preservation to food, and therefore, to life. Light illuminates the path for those in the darkness and provides a beacon to set a direction towards safety.

Between these two sections, we learn that righteous living has a twofold purpose. One, it brings benefit to us personally, as seen in the Beatitudes. We are blessed by the righteousness we live. Second, salt and light show righteous living is not merely for "me," but it results in a better outcome for "us." The Ancient Near East cultures placed a much greater emphasis on the value of being part of a community, contrasted to our modern Western emphasis on individualism. That sense of belonging to something bigger than yourself adds significant weight to Jesus's words. We are part of a community, a bigger body of people that are directly impacted by the choices we make in our lives; therefore, we have a responsibility to behave in a way that benefits the collective and not just the individual.[2]

Coming to our focus passage, Jesus sheds light on a major purpose of His own teaching ministry, namely, calling His listeners back to the type of righteous living God has always intended. The Sermon on the Mount plays a key role in that this discourse draws the attention back to the Mosaic Law's original intent. He is reminding people what God has always expected of them, yet years of misunderstanding, misuse, and abuse have muddled that knowledge.

No doubt, such a call would have been seen as radical or extreme to some, and it is not difficult to imagine many listeners ridiculing Jesus's approach. Perhaps, then, in verses 17–20, Jesus is anticipating and addressing what many of the established teachers would argue against in His message. In so doing, He also gives necessary insight for Christians to know what to do with the Old Testament.

Jesus's Relationship to the Law

> Do not think that I have come to abolish the Law or the
> Prophets; I have not come to abolish them but to fulfill
> them (Matthew 5:17 ESV).

The section begins with Jesus clarifying the nature of His relationship to the Old Testament. Evidently, He knows that some would hear His exposition to follow and be concerned that His goal is to eradicate the divine code. This is evident from the word *abolish*. The Greek word καταλύω conveys the picture of a demolition process or dismantling of an object.[3] It is the same word Jesus will use in Matthew 24:2 to describe the future destruction of the temple by the Romans. It is certainly noteworthy that He reassures the original listeners that His goal is not to demolish any of this divine code they love and follow. Why would such an assurance be necessary? Perhaps it is another testimony of how far their contemporary understanding and treatment of the Law had deviated from God's original intent. What Jesus is about to say to them in the body of the sermon might sound so radical that it comes across as destructive instead of restorative. Yet, nothing they are about to hear is contradictory to the divine code.

Instead, He reveals that His actual purpose is to "fulfill" the Law. The word "fulfill" (πληρόω) has a literal meaning, "to make full,"[4] as in filling a water bottle all the way to the brim. In figurative terms, it is used in scripture to denote "completion of a period of time; to finish something; to bring a designed end to a prophecy, obligation, promise, or law." One might also say "fulfill" denotes bringing something to its fullest purpose. This wider scope of uses naturally leads us to ask what Jesus means, exactly, when He says His purpose is to "fulfill" the Law. It seems that three possible answers are most likely.

1. He would literally do the things laid down in scripture.
2. He would bring out the full meaning and intention of scripture.
3. His life and teaching would bring scripture to completion or a designed end.

Perhaps a good argument can be made that Jesus would fulfill the Law in multiple ways. For one, He never violated one command.[5] Secondly, in addition to expounding on the Law's original intentions with the Sermon on the Mount, Jesus regularly clarified these intentions throughout his ministry.[6] Thirdly, His death, burial, and resurrection functioned as the necessary sacrifice that ratified a new covenant enacted on the Day of Pentecost,[7] thus bringing the Mosaic era to an end. As one commentator put it,

> Jesus does not merely affirm that He will maintain them. As He sees it, His task is to actualise the will of God made known in the Old Testament. He has come in order that God's Word may be completely fulfilled, in order that the full measure appointed by God Himself may be reached in Him. His work is an act of obedience also and specifically in the fact that He fulfils God's promise, cf. Matthew 3:15. He actualises the divine will stated in the Old Testament from the standpoint of both promise and demand.[8]

Additionally, Craig Blomberg adds, "Now Christ makes clear that He is not contradicting the law, but neither is He preserving it unchanged. He comes 'to fulfill' it, i.e., He will bring the law to its intended goal."[9]

The Enduring Authority of Scripture

> For truly, I say to you, until heaven and earth pass away, not an iota, not a dot, will pass from the Law until all is accomplished. Therefore, whoever relaxes one of the least of these commandments and teaches others to do the same will be called least in the kingdom of heaven, but whoever does them and teaches them will be called great in the kingdom of heaven (Matthew 5:18–19).

To further emphasize the point of verse 17, Jesus continues by reiterating the enduring, absolute authority of all scriptures, down to the smallest details. Notice, first, the emphasis on the continuous nature of scripture: "Until heaven and earth pass away." This is a reference to the created order of the universe. There is coming a day when, according to 2 Peter 3:10–13, this material world will be "burned up and dissolved," giving way to a new heaven and new earth. This means, according to our focus text, that God's divine scriptures possess absolute authority for all time. The one qualifier is "until all is accomplished." Blomberg, again, describes the point well.

> With the coming of Christ, many aspects of the law are brought to complete fruition (e.g., the need for sacrifices, on which see Hebrews). In other instances, certain requirements of the law endure until Christ's coming again (e.g., classically, love of neighbor and God).[10]

Jesus also emphasizes the fact that details matter in

scripture. "Iota" and "dot" refer to the smallest components of individual words in the ancient languages of the day. We might compare them to a "comma or apostrophe." Such markings could often be seen as insignificant to the point that many fail to appreciate their value to the language (evidenced by the lack of modern grammatical skills). Again, this reiterates His assertion earlier that He had not come to "abolish" any element of the divine code. Not one piece of the Law was deemed unnecessary or insignificant. In fact, Jesus goes on in verse 19 to boldly proclaim that one's dealings with the smallest of details would have a major impact on their status in the kingdom of heaven.

The ESV uses the word "relaxes" to translate the term λύση, which more literally means "to undo, loose, or tie." [11] In this context, it seems the message is not merely a warning against breaking the smallest of details, but rather setting them aside as though they are no longer applicable. Jesus wants His listeners to fully understand that it is unacceptable to disregard any element of God's holy scriptures. Those who are great in the kingdom are those who treat all of it with the utmost seriousness and respect.

Exceeding Righteousness

> For I tell you, unless your righteousness exceeds that of the scribes and Pharisees, you will never enter the kingdom of heaven (Matthew 5:20).

The final verse in our text finds Jesus naming a new demographic, which has probably been alluded to previously, that being the scribes and Pharisees. In His day, these two religious personalities set the standard for what religious living looked like. They were the ones people sought to emulate in matters of spirituality—the consummate rule keepers who strove for strict legal correctness. It is noteworthy that Jesus does not correct this particular trait about their approach to scripture, per se. In fact, it seems He has an appreciation for their attention to detail, especially when you consider His previous statements. However, there was clearly something missing, for Jesus challenges His listeners to have a righteousness which "exceeds that of the scribes and Pharisees!" No doubt this was a shocking bar to the minds of those listening. In terms of law keeping, who could possibly surpass the ones who were so particular even in their tithing of mint and cumin?[12]

The answer lies in the fact that Jesus speaks of a different kind of righteousness of grace through faith in love that is central to the Christian gospel. It is not earned by meticulous, legalistic law-keeping. And yet,

> This does not mean cheap grace, for the words of this verse bring out the truth that those who have been touched by Jesus live on a new plane, a plane in which the keeping of God's commandments is important. Their righteousness is a given righteousness .... But when he is given that standing, Jesus looks to him to live in accordance with that standing .... The Pharisees put a tremendous emphasis on the letter of the law, but Jesus was looking for something very different from the Pharisaic standard. For them it was a matter of observing regulations (and softening them where possible), but for him it was keeping the commandments in depth; he taught a radical obedience.[13]

In other words, Jesus needs His followers to understand that divine grace compels us to live in true discipleship of the heart, soul, mind, and strength[14] with a godliness that is undergirded and informed by the authority of the scriptures.

APPLICATION

As noted in the introduction, Matthew 5:17–20 has implications for two major questions that Christians must wrestle with regarding scripture. 1) Is the spirit or the letter of the law to be preferred? 2) What are we to do with the Old Testament in the New Testament era? Let us begin with the latter.

Contextually, keep in mind that Jesus is commenting on the Mosaic Law and Prophets as the historical reference to "scripture." The same could be said for other New Testament authors who are writing in the time before the full penning of the New Testament. Thus, we can see how this passage has some major implications for Christians and the way we treat and interpret the whole of scripture, especially the Old Testament. While we may think this is easy to answer, historically, Christians have not been able to find a uniform answer to the question. Interpretation efforts have ranged from allegorical to type-antitype, or some other form of symbolism.[15] Some Christian thought has been very dismissive of the Old Testament, basically rejecting it fully because "we are not under it anymore." Yet, the New Testament affirms that the Old Testament remains normative and relevant to followers of Jesus,[16] despite being under a new covenant. Furthermore, we have already noted how Jesus affirms the absolute authority of all scripture, down to the smallest, most seemingly insignificant of pieces. So, what is the answer?

The answer lies in Jesus. We can only understand how

to rightly interpret scripture when we understand how it has been fulfilled by Christ, who came to fulfill and accomplish the whole of it. Every Old Testament text must ultimately be viewed in light of Jesus's person, ministry, and the changes He introduced when He inaugurated the New Covenant.[17] This follows Jesus's own pattern of teaching employed with the disciples on the road to Emmaus. "And beginning with Moses and all the Prophets, he interpreted to them in all the Scriptures the things concerning himself." [18] Some elements are brought to fruition immediately (i.e., sacrifices). Some requirements in the Law endure until He comes again (i.e., love neighbor & God).

In short, Christian application of the Old Testament must always take into account both the continuities and the discontinuities with the New Testament. Given this hermeneutic, correct teaching and practice of all "these commandments" (v. 19, almost certainly referring back to the Old Testament law just mentioned) are crucial.

What about His question regarding the spirit and the letter? Which one is Jesus concerned with? The answer is, "Both!" As disciples of the Messiah, we must heed the instructions and warnings of the one we profess allegiance to. If He is concerned with the iotas and dots, the smallest of details, then we must be concerned with those as well. Yet, we must express a righteousness that exceeds the legalistic minutia of the scribes and Pharisees who missed "the weightier matters of the law: justice and mercy and faithfulness,"[19] out of a misguided sense of merited righteousness. Our task is to understand the bigger picture and intention of holiness that God expects from all who follow Him, not merely check items in a checklist of codes and deeds. True discipleship demands that we understand the heart of the divine code, while also practicing a fierce obedience to the Lord of Lords.

CONCLUSION

As long as the sun rises and sets, God's holy scriptures will have authority over the lives of humanity. As disciples of Jesus, we are compelled and obligated to be intimately familiar with the contents of those scriptures. Yet, it is not just knowledge of the content, but a faith-rooted commitment to "[store] up your word in my heart, that I might not sin against you."[20] This results in us being concerned with both the spirit and letter of the Law, and acknowledging the relevance of ALL scripture to our lives as we view it through the lens of Jesus's salvific work.

DISCUSSION QUESTIONS

1. Which do you tend to gravitate more towards: the spirit or the letter of the law?
2. How do we determine which things listed in the Old Testament are binding today in the New Testament era?
3. Which way(s) do you think is best to understand Jesus as "fulfilling" the Old Testament?
4. How does one use Jesus as the lens to read the Old Testament? What specific examples can you think of?
5. Do you agree that restorative efforts in spiritual scenarios are often interpreted as an attempt to

destroy that spiritual foundation? If so, why do people see it in this way?

6. How should Christians go about paying attention to the small details of the word of God without sliding into an overbearing, legalistic attitude like that of the Pharisees?

Endnotes

[1] Rom 6:14 ESV

[2] For a good discussion of this concept, see Joseph H. Hellerman, *When the Church Was a Family* (Nashville: B&H, 2009), 13–33.

[3] BDAG, s.v. "καταλύω."

[4] BDAG, s.v. "πληρόω."

[5] c.f. Hebrew 4:15.

[6] For Example: Mark 2:27; Matthew 22:36–40.

[7] Acts 2.

[8] Gerhard Kittel, "πληρόω," TDNT. E-Book from Olive Tree Software.

[9] *Matthew*, (Nashville: B&H, 1992), E-Book from Olive Tree Software.

[10] *Matthew*.

[11] BDAG, s.v. "λύω."

[12] Matthew 23:23.

[13] Leon Morris, *Matthew*, (Grand Rapids: Eerdmans, 1992). E-Book from Olive Tree Software.

[14] Mark 12:30.

[15] For a good summation, see Keith Stanglin, *The Letter and Spirit of Biblical Interpretation: From the Early Church to Modern Practice*, (Grand Rapids: Baker, 2018).

[16] 2 Timothy 3:16.

[17] Note, this does not negate the value of under-

standing Old Testament passages in their original context. Rather, this helps us understand how we are to utilize them in the New Testament era.

[18] Luke 24:27.
[19] Matthew 23:23.
[20] Psalm 119:11.

BIBLIOGRAPHY

Blomberg, Craig L. *Matthew*. New America Commentary, vol. 22. Nashville: B&H, 1992. E-Book edition from Olive Tree Software.

Danker, Frederick W., Walter Bauer, William F. Arndt, and F. Wilbur Gingrich. *Greek-English Lexicon of the New Testament and Other Early Christian Literature.* 3rd ed. Chicago: University of Chicago Press, 2000. E-Book edition from Olive Tree Software.

ESV. English Standard Version, Crossway, 2011.

Hellerman, Joseph H. *When the Church Was a Family: Recapturing Jesus' Vision for Authentic Christian Community.* Nashville: B&H, 2009.

Kittel, Gerhard, and Gerhard Friedrich, eds. *Theological Dictionary of the New Testament.* Translated by G. W. Bromiley. 10 vols. Grand Rapids: Eerdmans, 1964. E-Book edition from Olive Tree Software.

Morris, Leon. *Matthew*. The Pillar New Testament Commentary. Grand Rapids: Eerdmans, 1992. E-Book edition from Olive Tree Software.

Stanglin, Keith D. *The Letter and Spirit of Biblical Interpretation: From the Early Church to Modern Practice.* Grand Rapids: Baker, 2018.

ANGER

MATTHEW 5:20–30

DON SNODGRASS

We live in an angry world. From the time that Cain murdered Abel, humans have lived in an angry world. In our current society, we are bombarded with examples of anger. The most recent presidential elections in the United States (2020 and 2024) resulted in a lot of anger being demonstrated by members of each of the major political parties when their respective candidate lost the election. We see video clips of a parent rushing onto the wrestling mat at a junior league wrestling match, assaulting a referee because he made a call against their child. Some of the outrage and venom spewed on various forms of social media can be sickening. We read headlines of road rage instances resulting in one human being killing another human being because they felt they had been disrespected. Let's pause a moment and think—we actually created the term Road Rage for this behavior because it has become so rampant in our society. Yes, we live in an angry world.

But Jesus knew this. He knew that anger begins as an emotion which, if left unchecked, can lead to dangerous consequences. Jesus addressed our issue with anger during the Sermon on the Mount.

> For I tell you, unless your righteousness exceeds that of the scribes and Pharisees, you will never enter the kingdom of heaven. You have heard that it was said to those of old, "You shall not murder; and whoever murders will be liable to judgment." But I say to you that everyone who is angry with his brother will be liable to judgment; whoever insults his brother will be liable to the council; and whoever says, "You fool!" will be liable to the hell of fire. So if you are offering your gift at the altar and there remember that your brother has something against you, leave your gift there before the altar and go. First be reconciled to your brother, and then come and offer your gift. Come to terms quickly with your accuser while you are going with him to court, lest your accuser hand you over to the judge, and the judge to the guard, and you be put in prison. [Matthew 5:20—25][1]

Jesus knows that harboring anger in our hearts has the potential to harm us—mentally, physically, and most importantly, spiritually.

The phrase "refusing to forgive is like drinking poison and expecting the other person to die" is often attributed to Nelson Mandela. And while the origins of the quote have been debated, the importance of the message is its suggestion that the person who refuses to forgive is the one who suffers the most, while the person or situation they are angry with is often unaffected and perhaps even unaware.

The negative emotional and mental effects of holding onto one's anger can include increased stress and anxiety, depression and feelings of worthlessness, resorting to alcohol and/or drug abuse as coping mechanisms, and damage to one's relationships with family and friends, leading to feelings of isolation and loneliness.[2]

Some of the negative physical effects of unresolved anger can include the triggering of certain stress hormones, leading to a decline in heart health and a higher risk of heart attacks. Research has shown that anger can have an effect on the autonomic nervous system, including the digestive system, and can lead to unpleasant symptoms in gastrointestinal tract (including abdominal pain, stomach upset, and diarrhea), and over the longer term, chronic stress has been linked to the development of inflammatory bowel disease (IBD), irritable bowel syndrome (IBS), and gastroesophageal reflux disease (GERD). Additionally, unresolved anger can negatively affect a person's ability to get good sleep, which can cause a host of negative physical consequences.[3]

And while Jesus is concerned about our overall well-being, the context of Matthew 5:20–25 leads us to conclude that our spiritual well-being is at the heart of His words. As He said in verse 20, as His disciples, we are called to a righteousness that exceeds that of the scribes and Pharisees—one that challenges not only our physical actions, but also our way of thinking.

The Apostle Paul may shed a bit of light as to why this is important with respect to how we manage anger. In Ephesians 4:26, Paul writes, "Be angry and do not sin; do not let the sun go down on your anger." From this, I would suggest that Paul (and Jesus) knew that we cannot live lives totally absent from anger, but that we can control how we respond and express our anger. In this verse, we are encouraged to deal with our anger quickly—before the setting of the sun. In the following verse, Paul also explains why resolving our anger issues is so important—so that we do not provide the devil with an opportunity to set us against one another. How many marriages might have been saved, how many congregational splits might have been avoided if Paul's words had been followed?

Knowing that we should control our anger and resolve our conflicts is one thing, but how do we put this into practice?

In his book, *The Peacemaker: A Biblical Guide to Resolving Personal Conflict*,[4] Ken Sande provides four things to keep in mind when working to resolve conflict with someone and bring about reconciliation. He calls these the Four G's.

The first G is to Glorify God. When the Apostle Paul encouraged the Christians in Corinth to "do all to the glory of God" (1 Corinthians 10:31), he was not limiting this to praising God during their worship, but to honor and glorify God in their daily activities, especially when there was disagreement among them.

Before we begin trying to resolve our issue with a brother or sister, we need to pause and reflect on how we can honor and please the Lord in this situation. Some of the ways we can do this are by obeying Him and following His example. To keep this goal foremost in our minds as we strive to resolve the conflict, it may be helpful to frequently ask ourselves, "How can I please and honor the Lord in this situation?"

The second G is Get the Log Out of Your Own Eye. In the latter part of the Sermon on the Mount, when Jesus said, "You hypocrite, first take the plank out of your own eye, and then you will see clearly to remove the speck from your brother's eye," (see Matthew 7:5) He provided us with one of the most challenging principles, yet one of the most disarming tools for resolving conflicts. When we honestly ask ourselves how we have contributed to the conflict, then articulate this with humility to the other person(s), the chances of successfully coming to a resolution have been greatly increased.

The third G is Gently Restore. Another key principle for resolving conflicts is to help others understand how they have contributed to the conflict. When we think of how the other person has offended us, we often think of Jesus's words in Matthew 18:15: "If your brother sins against you, go and tell him his fault, between you and him alone." Yet we must continue to keep the first two G's in mind as we do this. It may be helpful to recall that Matthew recorded the parable of the Lost Sheep just before the instruction in 18:15 and to keep in mind the metaphor of a loving and gentle shepherd who goes looking for a wandering sheep. We should keep in mind that our goal is reconciliation, not to force others to admit that they have wronged us. While the verses following 18:15 do provide instructions for what to do if our initial approach is not successful, our goal still remains the same—reconciliation.

The fourth G is Go and be Reconciled. As Christians, we have experienced the greatest forgiveness and reconciliation in the world. Despite this, we often fail to show genuine forgiveness to others. When the Apostle Peter asked Jesus if forgiving someone seven times was enough, Jesus responded with the parable of the Unforgiving Servant (Matthew 18:21–35). The parable tells us of a servant who owed his king a debt so great that it would be impossible to pay. He begged for mercy, and the king forgave the debt. Later, this same servant found a fellow servant who owed him a much smaller debt, yet when he was asked to be merciful, he refused to forgive this comparatively insignificant debt and had his fellow servant put in debtors' prison. When the king learned of his servant's actions, he angrily rebuked him and had him put in debtors' prison until he could pay his impossible debt. Jesus's warning in verse 35 should make us tremble at the very thought of withholding forgiveness from someone.

Sande suggests that we use Four Promises of Forgiveness as we try to imitate God's forgiveness.

1. "I will not dwell on this incident."
2. "I will not bring up this incident again and use it against you."
3. "I will not talk to others about this incident."
4. "I will not let this incident stand between us or hinder our personal relationship."**

**Please note that this fourth promise does not at all suggest that someone must return to a dangerous or abusive relationship as a demonstration of forgiveness.

Just as we have been forgiven and reconciled for our offenses to God, we should seek reconciliation. Whether we are the offender (Matthew 5) or the one who has been offended (Matthew 18), we should seek out the other person with the goals of forgiveness and reconciliation. Don't you think it would put a smile on His face if two brothers were to meet each other on their way to putting His words into practice and seeking reconciliation with each other?

DISCUSSION QUESTIONS

1. According to Matthew 5:20, Jesus told the crowd that unless their righteousness exceeded

that of the scribes and Pharisees, they would never enter the kingdom of heaven. What do you think He was telling them? What does that mean to us today?

2. Read Matthew 5:21–22. Do you think Jesus is describing different forms or levels of anger and their consequences?

3. Why do we find resolving conflicts difficult? What keeps us from following Jesus's instructions about reconciling with one another?

4. Read Matthew 18:1–4. As you envision this event in your mind's eye, do you see any personal conflict between Jesus's disciples? Jesus once again warns of something that would prevent them from entering the kingdom of heaven. This time, it is become like children. What do you think this means, and how might that apply to resolving conflicts with one another?

5. As you read this chapter, was there someone who came to mind? Is there someone who feels you have wronged them in some way? Is there someone whom you feel has wronged you? What do you plan to do?

Endnotes

[1] All scripture references are from the English Standard Version unless stated otherwise.

[2] "How Unresolved Anger Impacts Mental Health: Recognizing the Signs and Seeking Help," Greater Boston Behavioral Health, https://greaterbostonbehavioralhealth.

com/rehab-blog/how-unresolved-anger-impacts-mental-health/

[3] "5 Ways Anger Affects Your Health," Everyday Health Group, https://www.everydayhealth.com/news/ways-anger-ruining-your-health/

[4] Ken Sande, *The Peacemaker: A Biblical Guide to Resolving Personal Conflict*, 3rd edition (Grand Rapids, MI: Baker Books, 2004).

Matthew 6:1–4

Eric Waller

Beware of practicing your righteousness before men to be noticed by them; otherwise you have no reward with your Father who is in heaven. So when you give to the poor, do not sound a trumpet before you, as the hypocrites do in the synagogues and in the streets, so that they may be honored by men. Truly I say to you, they have their reward in full. But when you give to the poor, do not let your left hand know what your right hand is doing, so that your giving will be in secret; and your Father who sees what is done in secret will reward you (NASB).

One Main Thing

It's no secret that we like to be accepted and applauded by others. The clothes we wear, our hairdo and make-up, our cars, our homes, and even our behaviors scream for social acceptance. They also frequently betray our lack of contentment with God's approval. Sometimes, even our time of arrival at church, the pew we sit on, or our volunteerism within the church are cries for recognition from others. It is as if God's endorsement is somehow insufficient. Christ, however, calls us to the higher standard of transparent faith and worship where our motive is pleasing God and receiving his approbation. He seeks a devout heart even if He alone witnesses it. Intimacy with Him excludes all attempts to receive the praise of others.

INTRODUCTION

Matthew 6:1–4 cannot be properly understood without considering its context within the Sermon on the Mount. To that end, one will note Matthew 5 ends with a call to spiritual completeness that rises above religious and cultural standards. In Matthew 6:1, Jesus begins a complementary discourse on the sincerity of one's faith and worship that is also a call to rise above earthly and religious tradition and culture. Throughout His sermon, Jesus repeatedly urges his hearers to adopt a spiritual perspective, to seek His mindset, and to disavow prevailing practices and perspectives that hinder a pure heart from sincerely responding to Him. Jesus's words are terse and offensive to some, but His purpose is to direct hearers to a deeper level of engagement with Him. Jesus also expands on this portion of His sermon in the verses following our text (6:5–18).

GOING DEEPER

Jesus begins Matthew 6 with an imperative, "*beware*." This is not a suggestion but a command. He commands examination of our own worship and faith to guard against it becoming an activity of self-aggrandizement. This term is used by Jesus elsewhere in Matthew's Gospel to prevent the deception of false prophets (7:15, 10:17) and to deter the corrupting legalism of the Pharisees and Sadducees (16:6, 11–12). The intent of *"beware"* is to self-examine, guard, and give close attention to our motives.

The issue of concern is that our otherwise righteous acts may be engaged in only to impress others (Matthew 6:1). If such occurs, then our works and worship are worthless, and we *"have no reward"* (Matthew 6:1). Performing spiritual acts of righteousness *"before men"* is not the issue. It is performing them before men for the wrong reason that raises Jesus's concerns. In this sermon, Jesus says that we *will* be observed by others and *ought* to be witnessed by others as we let our spiritual lights shine (Matthew 5:16). He also acknowledges that how and where we engage in spiritual activities can sometimes result in self-harm (Matthew 7:6). The directive then, is to *"beware"* when *"before men"* to ensure our efforts are not driven by attempts to impress others or *"to be noticed by them"* (6:1).

After giving this generalized introductory statement in Matthew 6:1, Jesus addresses specific areas of concern. They include giving to the poor (6:2–4), prayer (6:5–15), and fasting (6:16–18). The underlying principle, of course, applies to any activity. It was customary for the Romans to sound a trumpet (comparable to our modern drum roll) to announce a financial gift to the city, after which the donor would be honored by having his/her name placed on a scroll hanging in public for all to admire. Jesus says the religious hypocrites similarly blew the trumpet in both the synagogue and in the streets (apparently adopting the Roman custom), not to herald one's service to God or out of sincere concern for the poor recipients, but *"that they may be honored by men"* (6:2). In such instances, Jesus said, *"they have received their reward"* (6:2), which means the full extent of their reward is limited to the momentary public recognition they receive. God offers them nothing because their act was not precipitated from a relationship with Him, and it was not presented to Him or to please Him but was done only to promote oneself in the eyes of others. This means the motivation of our worship has everything to do with whether God accepts it!

These insincere people stood praying on street corners and in synagogues *"so that they may be seen of men"* (6:5), and their prayers included *"meaningless repetition "* in hopes they would *"be heard for their many words"* (6:7). Similarly when fasting they would *"neglect their appearance so that they will be noticed by men"* (6:16). Jesus called them *"hypocrites"* (6:2, 5, 16).

In contrast to this false spirituality designed to garner the praise of others, Jesus appealed to privacy in one's spiritual expressions by saying to *"not let your left hand know what your right hand is doing"* and to give *"in secret"* (6:3–4). Similarly, Jesus calls for prayer to be *"in secret"* (6:6) and for fasting to be *"in secret"* while maintaining one's normal hygiene (6:17–18). Jesus notes for all three (giving, prayer, and fasting) the Father sees what happens in secret and rewards accordingly (6:4, 6, 18). The concept of a reward from God for sincere faith is a repetitive theme in the Gospel of Matthew (5:12, 46; 6:1, 2, 5, 16; 10:41, 42; 20:8). God covets our sincere devotion to Him and showers us with blessings as our loving Father.

APPLICATION

Does this text mean that one cannot prepare in advance for public worship, such as leading a prayer or presiding at the communion table? Does Jesus mean that if teaching or preaching, one should not consider the audience and choose words or examples appropriate for that audience so it will be better received? If making a financial donation, does Jesus intend that one should be so secretive that the gift is not deducted on one's tax return or is hidden from one's spouse? No, no, and no! The caution Jesus offers is first about one's heart and intentions. He is demanding we check ourselves first to see whether our *"righteousness"* is conducted in sincerity as part of one's devotion to God or is designed to receive praise from others. The former reaps eternal rewards, while the latter reward is limited to the transient praise of others.

This should inform a prudent person that there may be a time, a manner, and a place for all spiritual activities. For example, a gift can be made anonymously or privately, so others have no idea about it. Prayer and fasting are deeply personal, and there is probably no reason to ever tell others, except perhaps as a teaching example if done humbly. The apostle Paul often prayed for others and told them he was praying for them not to bolster his image but to encourage them (Romans 1:10; Ephesians 1:16; Philippians 1:4, 9; Colossians 1:3, 9). Our first priority is that our hearts are devoted to God, and all spiritual efforts evolve from being rooted in that adoration.

CONCLUSION

We like praise! Everyone wants to receive recognition for their accomplishments. Our relationship with God, however, is not enhanced by human acceptance or applause. Those seeking such receive no heavenly reward for their efforts. Jesus commands us to examine ourselves to be sure all of our spiritual actions are sincere and conducted without consideration of accolades from others. This reflects the deeply intimate relationship God demands between Himself and us. This is the higher standard to which Jesus calls us!

Discussion Questions

1. Does Jesus contradict Himself when He tells us to let our light shine before others (Matthew 5:16), but not to practice righteousness to be noticed by others (Matthew 6:1)? Why/Why not?

2. What are the two types of rewards mentioned in Matthew 6:1–4 and the primary differences in them?

3. Why does Jesus promote doing things "*in secret*" (Matthew 6:4)?

4. Does Jesus condemn engaging in public competitions for Bible knowledge, or judging people for their talents in preaching, song leading, or leading prayer?

5. What is the difference between praying a long prayer and in "*meaningless repetition*" (Matthew 6:7)?

6. What can we do to increase intimacy with God and dispel attempts to seek the praise of others in our practice of righteousness?

Pray Then Like This
Matthew 6:5–15
Joshua Pappas

Focus Passage

Matthew 6:5–15

One Main Thing

The Sermon on the Mount is the sermon of sermons! Surrounded by His closest disciples as well as multitudes of believers, seekers, questioners, and crowd-followers, Jesus set forth His way of life—*the* way of life that embodies the righteous intent of God's Law (Matthew 5:17–20). It begins with a seemingly paradoxical view of happiness in this world (5:2–12), proceeds into an unforgettable illustration of the influence of truth as salt, light, and a city set on a hill (5:13–16), and then offers an approach to behavior that is comprehensively Biblical, exposes hypocrisy, and weakens the power of temptations by guiding us to cut them off at their roots (5:21–48). As the sermon flows into Matthew 6, it provides a simple normative pattern for giving, fasting, and praying (6:1–18). After forbidding us to pray like

Jewish hypocrites or lawless Gentiles (6:5–8), Jesus simply says, "Pray then like this:"

> Our Father in heaven, hallowed be your name. Your kingdom come, your will be done, on earth as it is in heaven. Give us this day our daily bread, and forgive us our debts, as we also have forgiven our debtors. And lead us not into temptation, but deliver us from evil (Matthew 6:9–13).[1]

The Lord concludes the teaching about prayer with a warning that we must pray justly. If we seek forgiveness, we must give it (Matthew 6:14–15). It should be noted that the Lord's initial notes (6:5–8) also rule out the idea of "The Lord's Prayer" being a thing to memorize by rote and recite as an empty ritual. There's nothing wrong with praying His actual words, but we must mean them from the heart. "The model prayer" is an outline, a pattern—a "coatrack" of sorts, upon which we all can (and should) hang our own "garments."

Introduction

Praying is one of the most purely spiritual things we can do. While our prayers often focus on needs and concerns about life in this visible world, praying is reaching out spiritually to speak into the heaven we've never visited to talk to the God we've never seen. "For we walk by faith, not by sight" (2 Corinthians 5:7). Every man, woman, and child should pray to God and live a prayerful life. Nothing we can do is more powerful than praying, not because of any power in ourselves or in the act of praying, itself, but because the one we petition is the Almighty, who loves us, and has promised to answer (Matthew 7:7–8, John 16:23–24, 1 Peter 3:12, 1 John 5:14–15). Jesus's model prayer in Matthew 6 gives us a basic, versatile outline we can all use to structure our prayers in a way that honors God and that He will honor. Let's study it together.

GOING DEEPER

"Our Father in heaven."[2] Here, the Lord teaches us to call on His Father as "our" Father, and we should not take this for granted. Merely being human does not grant us the right to call on the God against Whom we have rebelled as Father (Ephesians 2:2, 5:6; Romans 8:15, 23; Galatians 4:5; Ephesians 1:5). All is not well for those outside of a covenant relationship with Christ. Only those who are in Christ have the right to call on God as Father (John 1:12–13).

It is interesting that this model prayer,[3] as presented by Matthew, is not individualistic. Jesus didn't instruct His hearers to say, "My Father in heaven," but "Our Father in heaven." Now, for the sake of teaching the whole counsel of God, I want us all to recognize that in Luke's account of the model prayer, Jesus does address the Father as if one-on-one (Luke 11:2). There's nothing sinful about starting a prayer with, "My Father," or simply, "Father ...." However, in Matthew's account, the prayer is communal for a reason. We need to understand that while we each, individually, have access to God's ear through Christ, we are never really praying alone, nor should we wish to be, but are praying as members of a community of believers—God's family. As we will see next, it's right to pray for our own needs and wants, but we should always pray with a heart that loves the brotherhood, remembering all the saints are in this together.

"Hallowed be Your name." May the Spirit help us never to forget whom we address in prayer. God is great above our ability to comprehend! He is the Creator and Author of Life, who is singularly responsible for providing us every good thing we've had, have, or ever will have (Acts 17:24–25, James 1:16–17). He is worthy of all praise, glory, and honor, and is not to be approached disrespectfully. "Access with boldness" (Ephesians 3:12) does not mean we forget "the fear of the Lord," which is fundamental to a proper prayer life (Proverbs 1:7). Do not forget that God "must be respected as holy" (Leviticus 10:3 ICB).

"Hallowed" means made or regarded as holy, and this is not merely a formal greeting, but a request that God will make it everywhere so. In other words, when we pray, "Hallowed be Your name," we're not only respecting His name, ourselves, but praying the time will come when everyone respects His name like they should. When Jesus became aware the hour of His suffering had come, He prayed, "'Father, glorify your name.' Then a voice came from heaven: 'I have glorified it, and I will glorify it again'" (John 12:28). Praying is participating in God's work to bring all creation into harmony with His will. Prayer is powerful! (James 5:16)

"Your kingdom come, your will be done, on earth as it is in heaven." Some teachers have stressed that since the kingdom of God came with power on Pentecost (Mark 9:1; Luke 24:49; Acts 1:8, 2:1–4) and that all the faithful are presently in it (Colossians 1:13), we ought not to speak these words in our prayers, today, the way Jesus instructed His hearers to do then. This is a misunderstanding. The kingdom of heaven has indeed come, initially, and all true believers are in it, but it has not yet come in the fullness that Jesus's model prayer is asking for. The modifier, "on earth as it is in heaven," applies to both preceding statements, "Your kingdom come," and "Your will be done." Both statements mean the same thing. We all ought to pray that life on this earth will reflect that of heaven more and more every day. The work of the Great Commission (Matthew 28:18–20, etc.) is the effort to make it so. God wants everyone to freely enter His kingdom, which means to submit to His will. To simplify, this means we ought to pray for the success of the gospel everywhere so that, to the fullest degree possible, every person on the planet will believe and obey it.

Following our offering God the praise He deserves and requesting that His mission be fully successful, Jesus teaches us to make requests for our physical needs and for spiritual guidance and strength. "Give us *this day* our *daily* bread" is time-specific. It means now—today—not tomorrow, next week, or next year. This lines up with the teaching just a few verses down in the context (Matthew 6:25ff), that concludes with, "Therefore do not be anxious about tomorrow, for tomorrow will be anxious for itself. Sufficient for the day is its own trouble" (6:34).

Our material needs are real. Jesus obviously approves of our asking for them in prayer. But our spiritual needs are incomparably more important. The model prayer concludes, "Forgive us our debts, as we also have forgiven our debtors. And lead us not into temptation, but deliver us from evil." (The original Greek can be translated, "Deliver us from the evil one.") There is nothing a sinner needs more than forgiveness, and the only people on the planet who aren't sinners are children (and the childlike) who haven't yet (or never will) come to an accountable understanding. Nevertheless, if this world continues long enough, children will eventually learn of sin the hard way (Romans 3:23). As baptized believers, forgiveness of sins is ours continually if we continue in the faith (1 John 1:7). Sins of rebellion, if persisted in, lead to apostasy (Hebrews 10:26–27). But all Christians commit sins of ignorance and weakness that, though inexcusable (1 Corinthians 10:12–13), do not cause us to be cut off from grace. Christians do not fall back into condemnation every time we fail! However, God wants us to confess our sins and ask for forgiveness. It's a matter of a genuine relationship to do so. We need to be transparent in our relationship with God. James wrote, "You do not have, because you do not ask" (James 4:2). If Jesus teaches us to ask for forgiveness, we ought to ask for forgiveness.

We desperately need to be delivered from evil in all its forms, including the temptations that arise from within our own hearts (James 1:13–14). We especially need deliverance from the attention and devices of the evil one, Satan. Thankfully, we know "He who is in [us] is greater than he who is in the world" (1 John 4:4). If Jesus teaches us to ask, and He's promised we have what we ask for (John 15:7), then, by praying according to the model prayer, we can live with certainty that we are protected from Satan!

Even though none of us will be altogether without temptations in this life, and all suffer various troubles, the model prayer assures us that God will fully protect us from evil. We can thus know that when some evil comes our way, it is known to God, and God will walk with us through it to His glory and our ultimate betterment (Hebrews 13:5). We can rightly say all trials and temptations are opportunities to glorify God. Through prayer, we have every reason to rejoice in our tribulations (Romans 5:1–5). Prayer is one of the blessings that make the Christian life the good life. We can hold our heads high no matter what because of the gift of our Savior's model prayer.

APPLICATION

1. Pray with reverence. Begin your prayers by acknowledging God's holiness. Reflect on His greatness and majesty until you develop the appropriate awe and respect. As a rule, start each prayer by praising God before presenting your requests. God is worthy of praise!

2. Pray for God's will and mission. Pray for God's kingdom to advance and His will to be done. Regularly pray for the spread of the gospel, the growth of the church, and for unbelievers to come to faith. This aligns our hearts' desires with God's eternal purpose.

3. Cultivate a communal prayer mindset. Jesus's use of "our" Father emphasizes praying as part of God's family. Make it a habit to pray for other believers' needs, such as healing, strength, and wisdom, alongside your own, whether in personal prayer or group settings.

4. Trust God for your daily needs. The request for "daily bread" encourages us to learn to rely on God for provision in real time. This will strengthen our faith. Jesus's example is of owning nothing more than the clothes on His back, and the Father provided for Him every day. Do we trust Him? Apply this by praying specifically for today's needs—physical, emotional, and relational—trying not to worry so much about tomorrow. God is faithful! There's nothing wrong with a savings account, and the Bible bears this out, but too many of us

are far too burdened with worrying about a
future that may never come.

5. Seek forgiveness and extend it. Regularly
confess your sins to God, as Jesus instructs, and
ask for forgiveness to maintain a transparent
relationship with Him. Equally, forgive others
who have wronged you, reflecting God's grace
in your relationships. Seek reconciliation with
anyone you've held a grudge against or who
may have something against you (Matthew
5:24, Luke 17:3).

6. Ask for spiritual protection. Pray for
deliverance from temptation and evil, trusting
God to guide and protect you. Ask for strength
to resist specific temptations you face and for
discernment to recognize Satan's schemes.
Never forget that God is infinitely more
powerful than the devil.

7. Develop a consistent prayer routine. Spiritual
life is best lived in rhythm. Jesus's model prayer
is simple, versatile, and meant for regular use.
Create a daily prayer habit using it as an outline
—praise, God's will, provision, forgiveness,
protection—to structure your prayers.

CONCLUSION

In Matthew 6:5–15, Jesus provides a timeless model for
prayer that is both profoundly simple and deeply spiritual.
It guides us to connect with God as "Our Father" in a way
that He will honor. This prayer is not a rote formula to
recite ritually, but a versatile framework for expressing
reverence, celebrating communal faith, and trusting in

God's provision, forgiveness, and protection. By teaching us to pray for God's name to be hallowed, His kingdom to come, and our needs—both physical and spiritual—to be met, Jesus invites us into a life of confident, faith-filled dependence on the Almighty. Through this model, we who believe are empowered to pray humbly and boldly, knowing that God hears and answers our prayers according to His perfect will. A consistent prayer life will always strengthen our relationship with God and deepen our unity with fellow believers.

DISCUSSION QUESTIONS

1. How does starting our prayers with "Hallowed be Your name" shape our attitudes toward God and influence the way we approach prayer? Can you share an example of how praising God first has impacted your prayer life?

2. Jesus emphasizes praying as a community with "Our Father" rather than "My Father" in Matthew's account. How can we practically incorporate praying for the needs of other believers into our daily prayer routines, and why is this communal focus important?

3. The request for "daily bread" encourages trusting God for immediate needs without worrying about the future. What are some practical ways we can cultivate this trust, especially during times of uncertainty or lack?

4. The model prayer includes asking for forgiveness and deliverance from temptation. How does regularly confessing our sins and

praying for spiritual protection strengthen our relationship with God and our ability to overcome life's challenges?

ENDNOTES

[1] All Scripture references are from the English Standard Version (ESV) unless otherwise specified.

[2] I do not think believers are forbidden to pray to God the Son or God the Holy Spirit. There are clear examples in the New Testament of believers praying to Jesus (Acts 7:59–60, 9:10–16; 2 Corinthians 12:8–9; Revelation 22:20; cf. John 14:8–11). However, some strongly disagree, and I respect their convictions. There is at least enough evidence in Scripture to justify praying to the "Second" and "Third" Persons of the Trinity to support us all remaining unified as brothers and sisters in Christ in good standing, even if we disagree about this, because we can all agree that the general or usual New Testament pattern for prayer is to address God the Father in the name of God the Son (John 16:23–24), relying on the intercession of the Holy Spirit (Romans 8:26).

[3] Even if God allows some of us to be persecuted to the death, He will restore us to eternal life and endless blessings so that, in the end, evil will have utterly failed to do us lasting harm (2 Corinthians 1:10).

Relational Dynamics Revealed in the Model Prayer for Faithful Living

Matthew 6:9–13

Michael Farris

FOCUS PASSAGE

In this manner, therefore, pray: Our Father in heaven, hallowed be Your name. Your kingdom come, your will be done on earth as it is in heaven. Give us this day our daily bread. And forgive us our debts, as we forgive our debtors. And do not lead us into temptation, but deliver us from the evil one. For Yours is the kingdom and the power and the glory forever. Amen (Matthew 6:9–13 NKJV).

ONE MAIN THING

Our relationships are crucial to the life we live. The closer those relations align with God's design, the greater the blessing. God intends for us to be blessed, not merely by our fellowship with humankind, but especially with Him.

GOING DEEPER

During His ministry, Jesus presented the renowned *Sermon on the Mount*. Let's focus on what some call *The Model Prayer* (Matthew 6:9–13) and see how crucial relational dynamics are revealed in each clause.

"Our Father in heaven" reveals the **Father/child** dynamic. Here, the word *father* is a translation of the word *Abba* and contains intimate feelings of familial closeness. We should be as stunned as they were to hear of this relational dynamic. The Almighty wants a perfectly blessed Father/Child relationship with us. Wow!

As creator, He is our source of origin. As the architect behind the plan for our redemption, He loved us long before we understood His sacrifice for our salvation. We are all His children by creation, but sin damaged that precious relationship. God left Heaven to live as a human to die for us. That's one extent to which He has already shown us His love as a perfect Father. So now the question is whether we choose to belong to God by redemption through His Son.

Notice how these facts link together. The Son of God (the Word of God) IS God (John 1). Jesus is God in the Flesh: The Messiah (the chosen, anointed sacrificial Lamb of heaven). He is Lord, King of Kings, who becomes Savior to those reborn by baptism into Him. That's when Jesus, the Lord Himself, becomes our brother. This spiritual rebirth places us into the heavenly family, where the Lord, God's Son, is now a sibling. As His redeemed children, we can approach God as "Father!" (1 Peter 5:7) How wonderful that our God, who rules the universe, gives each of His children the full attention, wisdom, and resources required for our maturation.

"Hallowed be your name" reveals the

God/worshipper dynamic. What an incredible privilege to approach the sovereign ruler of the universe with acceptable worship. Isaiah's experience of His holiness (Isaiah 6:1–5) brought him to his knees in woeful distress by contrast, realizing that only God is holy, righteous, and worthy of all worship. We need to be like the creatures and elders in Revelation 4:9–11 who discarded their golden crowns in the presence of the holy Lord. If we think anything gives us a claim to worthiness, we must be willing to yield it all to the honor of God's absolute worthiness. He is God; we are the worshippers.

"**Your kingdom come; your will be done …**" reveals the **King/subject** dynamic. He is our **King,** and we are the **subjects**. He doesn't need our consent before ruling. He is the **ruler**, and we are the **ruled**. We are called to carry out His will, whatever it is. Many outside the kingdom initially have difficulty accepting Jesus, or anyone, as **master** if that implies they are the **servants**. Thankfully, He is a righteous king. In the context of prayer, Jesus spoke of His heavenly father as good, wise, and benevolent (Matthew 7:7–11). It is a joy to serve this good King. We know He will rule in a way that is best for us. As members of His church, Christians are citizens of His kingdom (Colossians 1:13), praying for it to increase as more people seek God's will for their lives.

"**Give us this day our daily bread**" reveals the **Provider/dependent** dynamic. Acts 17:25 presents a stunning truth about God and a humbling truth about ourselves. God is complete and needs nothing from us. Conversely, we have daily needs and fully depend on Him for all blessings. A popular story illustrates this. A scientist tells God, "With all we've discovered, we can do everything on our own, even make life." God says, "Try it." The scientist bends down to scoop some dirt when God says, "Wait! Get your own dirt." Without God manifesting His daily benevolence, we would have nothing, accomplish nothing, and be nothing. But the person we have become in Christ is a tribute of praise to the one who has sustained us all along.

"Forgive us our debts" reveals the **Creditor/debtor** dynamic. God is the **creditor** and humanity is the **debtor**. The debt humanity incurred against God is enormous (Romans 3:23, 6:23). The payment for our sin-debt would be eternal death. Sin is that *serious* because God is that *holy*. The only way my relationship with God can be restored is for someone entirely righteous to make atonement. But since every accountable human has incurred sin, who could qualify? There appears to be no hope for humanity. However, there is GREAT NEWS of a GLORIOUS GOSPEL (1 Timothy 1:11)! Paul wrote, in 2 Corinthians 5:14–15, how God Himself offers atonement through His incarnate Son's sinless sacrifice. The divine Word of God was willing and eager to enter His creation, to live as a human, with no sin to His name, to make atonement for all! Those redeemed rejoice in this forgiveness continually given, which motivates righteous living.

"As we also have forgiven our debtors" reveals the **Example/adherent** dynamic. In offering merciful forgiveness, God is our example. We must exhibit the same to our fellow man. Jesus tells of a forgiving king who settles accounts with his servants in Matthew 18:23–35. One servant owed 10,000 talents, an impossible sum to repay, but he begged for mercy, and the king granted it. The forgiven servant immediately went to find one who owed him 100 denarii. While demanding payment, he began to choke the man. These actions were justly reported to the king. The king was angry and revoked his mercy, now casting that servant into debtor's prison until he paid back the unpayable debt. That servant did not follow the example of his king. This servant did not show the king's mercy to his fellow servant.

"Lead us not into temptation" reveals the **Guide/follower** dynamic. God knows the terrain of our spiritual battlefields. He wants to guide us in avoiding/conquering temptations that threaten our relationship with Him. While the Lord hates sin, temptations will come. So, in our resolve to not displease the Lord, we must seek His guidance to overcome.

"But deliver us from evil" reveals the **Deliverer/freed-captive** dynamic. What is the heart of this model prayer about? The pinnacle of our spiritual lives, our greatest blessing, is SALVATION. Romans 6:16 teaches we are either slaves to sin or righteousness. As a slave to sin, those chains held us captive for a fate of eternal separation from God. But God delivered us! God delivers any who faithfully respond to His Son! (Acts 2:38) Being delivered from this condemnation makes it a joy to live faithfully to the one who grants me spiritual life.

APPLICATION

We can mature in this **Father/child dynamic** by acting like His reborn child. Jesus used a tough scenario earlier in His sermon (Matthew 5:44–45), to emphasize behaving like the Father strictly because we are His children. Rather than acting childish, we accept the role of maturing daily to think and behave more like our Father. This is often difficult. Unlike an immature child, pridefully rejecting a parent's essential assistance, a humble child is eager and grateful for the help offered. As we act like our Father, we proclaim that we are God's reborn child (John 8:44).

We can mature in this **God/worshipper** dynamic by practicing worship in the right spirit according to His revealed Truth. John 4:24 teaches worship is acceptable if in the right spirit according to truth! John 17:17 teaches that God's very Word is truth. Amazingly, 1 Peter 5:6 teaches the Most-High Lord exalts those who exalt Him. So, for every good reason, we want to offer appropriate worship.

We can mature in this **King/subject** dynamic by obeying Him. In Matthew 22:21, Jesus gives profound advice to those asking about the poll tax. The coin was Caesar's because it had Caesar's image on it. Since we have God's image upon us, let us give God what is His. Commit our lives to learning and living by His Word (Romans 10:17).

We can mature in this **Provider/dependent** dynamic by remembering we utterly depend on God to supply our needs. Beyond our physical needs, God supplies the needs of our eternal souls. 1 John 4:4 and 5:4 teach that God will help His children conquer sin and overcome temptation. In 2 Corinthians 12:7–10, Paul correctly assesses his struggles and victories. Paul knew he could only appropriate this divine blessing of God's strength and wisdom by fully, humbly depending on Him. How does this play out in our lives? Since our heavenly Father knows our feelings and frustrations (Psalm 31:7, 56:8, 103:13), our response must *cast our care on Him* as He graciously commands (1 Peter 5:7). Since He knows our faults and failures (Psalm 69:5), our response must be sheer honesty, with God and ourselves (1 John 1:8). Since He knows our fears (Matthew 6:31–33), our response must be to trust Him (Philippians 4:6). Since He knows our future (Psalm

139:16), our response should be to seek His guidance (Jeremiah 33:3). Since He knows the faithfulness of His children (Matthew 6:1, 4), our response is the confident resolve to live a life of joyful praise because we know He sees! (Galatians 6:9)

We can mature in this **Creditor/debtor** dynamic by thinking often about the gospel's greatest exchange. Titus 2:11–14 explains that, in our baptism, God canceled *our sin* for *His righteousness*. Jesus sacrificed His life so we could live. Let this truth motivate faithfulness to Jesus's righteousness (Ephesians 2:10).

We can mature in this **Example/adherent** dynamic by following God's example of mercy. To continue in the blessing of receiving this marvelous gift, we must share it as God has shown us.

We can mature in this **Guide/follower** dynamic by trusting the guide and obeying His instruction. While we journey in this sinful world, we won't always understand the depth or reason behind His instruction. That fact only emphasizes the point: to be delivered from temptation, listen to our guide. With Jesus as my good shepherd, He will lead us safely through (John 10:9–14, Psalm 23, Proverbs 3:5).

We can mature in this **Deliverer/freed-captive** dynamic by dwelling on our spiritual blessings in Christ (Ephesians 1:3–14), considering that we were atoned from a sin-debt too great for us to pay. We were delivered from the darkness of all evils to walk the righteous path of light (Romans 8:2–11). Having gotten the debt out of the way, He focuses on building us up into so much more. Being "saved by grace through faith" is the highest motivation to give God our all. Be motivated by Ephesians 3:20–21 to dream great goals for God.

Now to Him who is able to do exceedingly abundantly above all that we ask or think, according to the power that works in us, to Him be glory in the church by Christ Jesus to all generations, forever and ever. Amen.

Be inspired by 1 Chronicles 29:11 to praise and prioritize God in all you do. David praises God before the assembly,

Yours, O Lord, is the greatness and the power and the glory and the majesty and the splendor, for everything in heaven and earth is yours. Yours O Lord is the kingdom; you are exalted as head over all.

CONCLUSION

What an amazing God we serve! Let us embrace and mature in these life-changing, life-giving relational dynamics with our great God.

DISCUSSION QUESTIONS

1. What part does God's sovereignty play in the Lord's model prayer?
2. What petitions do we bring before the Father, and why do we rely on Him for them?
3. Is the model prayer intended to be used exactly by us today? Why or why not?
4. What does "Your will be done" mean for us today?
5. According to the model prayer, how does trusting in God lead to our spiritual growth?

6. What are several major points you see Jesus emphasizing in the Model Prayer?

GIVING DUE CREDIT

This content is my adaptation of a sermon outline by Edwin Crozier on Oct.16, 2011, in Kentucky at the Brownsburg Church of Christ. His primary source was written notes by Ken Weliever.

http://www.bburgchurchofchrist.org/media/sermons/2011/10/16/our-relationships-with-god-part-1

On Fasting

Matthew 6:16–18

Russell Wyatt

Focus Passage

Matthew 6:16–18 ESV

> And when you fast, do not look gloomy like the hypocrites, for they disfigure their faces that their fasting may be seen by others. Truly, I say to you, they have received their reward. But when you fast, anoint your head and wash your face, that your fasting may not be seen by others but by your Father who is in secret. And your Father who sees in secret will reward you.

Introduction

Several years ago, I attended the Youth Ministers Workshop at Graymere Church of Christ in Columbia, Tennessee, when I had my first big question on fasting. The workshop happened to be on my birthday, and the director at the time, Rusty Pettus, found out. He decided to give me a present: a book on the spiritual discipline of fasting. I was caught off guard by the surprise, and I remember saying thank you and jokingly adding, "Are you trying to say I'm fat?"

I had always dismissed fasting for the same reason many do: we do not often practice or teach about it in the United States. After all, the church in the US is the land of ice cream suppers, progressive dinners, and potlucks. We also say that breakfast is the most important meal of the day. That means that "breaking fasts" is just what we do.

As I read the book, my confidence in what I knew wavered. I thought about fasting like I never had before. Was fasting something that was just an old tradition? Or had I missed something important plainly stated in the scriptures because of my bias? I began to question if we were neglecting something important, something Biblical, and something that Jesus expected us to do. This became clear as I read the Sermon on the Mount.

GOING DEEPER

The text of Matthew 6:16–18 is part of the Sermon on the Mount. It is the foundation of our understanding of many of our Christian values. Jesus teaches us how to live with it. From this sermon, we learn about God and His expectations. We break down the foundational truths of worship, including prayer and giving. Fasting is included in this teaching and is located right next to those two with purpose.

Chapter 6 begins with Jesus teaching how people should avoid practicing their righteousness, that is, their righteous deeds before others to be seen by them (Matthew 6:1). This teaching groups three points: giving to the needy (6:2–4), prayer (6:5–15), and fasting (6:16–18). Note how Jesus starts with "Thus, when you ..." in verse 2 and couples prayer and fasting with the same statement, "And when you

..." in verses 5 and 16. These words show that fasting is joined with giving and praying. It even concludes with the reward for each of these being treasures in heaven (Matthew 6:19–20).

Giving to the needy is simple, and Jesus explains prayer in great detail, but what is fasting all about? Fasting is the act of denying yourself food. As a religious practice, it is not done for the reasons many people in our culture fast today. We often hear about fasting for weight loss, surgery preparation, or mental clarity. Where is God in that? When David fasted in 2 Samuel 1:11–12, when the church at Antioch fasted before sending Barnabas and Saul off on a mission in Acts 13:2–3, and when Barnabas and Paul fasted during the appointment of elders in the church in Acts 14:23, God is at the center of what is being done. Note that fasting is done with prayer in the two New Testament examples.

Fasting as a spiritual discipline in the scriptures is done for various reasons, including mourning, penitence, seeking divine deliverance, or because the person has a troubled spirit (*Lexham Bible Dictionary*). As mentioned in 2 Samuel 1:11–12, David's fasting was due to mourning. The one command for Israel to fast regularly in the Old Testament is on the Day of Atonement (Leviticus 16:29–31). The word there is often translated as "afflict yourself," sometimes "fasting." The idea is humbling one's soul in the form of self-denial. It would include fasting, but it may have even included more, such as abstaining from forms of self-pleasure or self-care (*NET Bible First Edition Notes*). Why would anybody do these things? A person would do this because it is an act of mourning, repentance, seeking divine deliverance, allowing for focus, or acknowledging one's dependence on God.

We can see why the hypocrites would be gloomy and try to look pitiful by disfiguring their faces. They want the attention of their peers. They want people to look at them and say, "See how righteous they are!" Jesus says, "Truly, I say to you, they have received their reward" (Matthew 6:16b). The attention and praise are their reward. Christ's instruction, like the others, takes it back to the private, personal devotion to God. He says that when we fast, we should do our best to hide it. It is not for others; it is between us and God. We should not self-promote by garnering pity or praise. God sees, and He will reward us. What reward? Remember those treasures we are laying up in heaven (Matthew 6:19–21)? That is the reward to which Jesus is pointing.

APPLICATION

Should we fast today? Yes. The New Testament provides examples of the spiritual discipline by churches and individuals. Even in our focus text, there is an underlying assumption that people will fast. Jesus does not say, "If you choose to," He says, "When you fast ...." Jesus expects people will be doing these things. Yet often, people see fasting as optional.

When and how should we fast? It does not need to be complicated. We often fast already without even thinking about it. What is the classic American Christian tradition when someone dies? Take the family food. Churches frequently provide food for families during times of distress. Perhaps this is because it is natural for people to abstain from food during times of mourning or other great stress, and we desire to look out for them. When we experience significant loss, often, people need to remind us to eat, and usually, that is the last thing we want to do.

There are times for fasting today, and we should take advantage of them. Sometimes, we should abstain from earthly pleasures, focus on the divine, and pray. It is not complicated; stop doing anything else and pray. And when we are hungry, we should use it as a reminder of why we are doing what we are doing.

There are also times we should feast in contrast to fasting. As Solomon wrote, "For everything there is a season, and a time for every matter under heaven ... a time to weep, and a time to laugh; a time to mourn, and a time to dance" (Ecclesiastes 3:1, 4). We mark our times of great joy and fellowship in the church with feasts of celebration, such as the youth group pizza party or a bridal shower potluck. In these moments, we should focus on God's blessings and thank Him for them. Jesus was accused by the Pharisees of wrongdoing when He and His disciples did not practice fasting. His answer shows us that there are appropriate times for both. Matthew 9:15 says, "And Jesus said to them, 'Can the wedding guests mourn as long as the bridegroom is with them? The days will come when the bridegroom is taken away from them, and then they will fast." They celebrated because Jesus was with them. Wouldn't you do the same?

CONCLUSION

Fasting and feasting are simple. Often, we lose the reason behind what we do and go on autopilot in what we see as the mundane. We lose sight of the divine in the rhythms of life.

Let us all be reminded that we are not our own but

belong to God (Romans 14:7–8). Everything we do, including fasting or feasting, should be done for Him. That is also why fasting should be a personal thing. While it can be done in groups (Acts 13:2–3), it should not be done to be seen by others. We should not be like the hypocrites. Let us lay up for ourselves treasures in heaven.

DISCUSSION

1. Name at least three biblical examples of reasons people fasted. Do people still do these today?
2. What are some reasons people may be resistant to fasting?
3. Is fasting easier or more acceptable in other cultures? Why or why not?
4. Read Matthew 6:1. Why is fasting an act of righteousness?
5. Consider fasting as a spiritual discipline like prayer or giving. What are the spiritual benefits of fasting?

MATTHEW 6:19–34

TRAVIS BOOKOUT

FOCUS PASSAGE

Matthew 6:19–34

INTRODUCTION

This passage is in the heart of the Sermon on the Mount. Jesus has been discussing a higher level of righteousness that should define His people and make them shine like lights of the world, stand out like a city on a hill, and improve the earth like salt in a dish. These goals will not happen by imitating the world. Jesus teaches a distinct righteousness elevated above the scribes and Pharisees (Matthew 5:20), the tax collectors (Matthew 5:46), the Gentiles (Matthew 5:47; 6:7, 32), and the hypocrites (Matthew 6:5, 16). Part of Jesus's kingdom mission in Matthew is the formation of a people unparalleled in righteousness.

While examples of this type of superior righteousness have already appeared regarding anger, lust, divorce, honesty, revenge, love, generosity, prayer, and fasting, Jesus now turns more specifically to wealth and money. Jesus is going to provide a helpful antidote to the plagues caused by a heart that pursues wealth. Christians should view and use money differently than the world.

GOING DEEPER

Matthew 6:19–34 breaks down into four major teachings: Matthew 6:19–21, 22–23, 24, and 25–34. Matthew 6:19–21 contrasts two imperatives. The first is a command not to store up treasure on earth, and the second is the command to store up treasure in heaven. These contrasting commands are both explained by parallel contrasting consequences. Treasures stored on earth do not last and are tainted with uncertainty and insecurity. Treasures stored in heaven, however, are guaranteed to be safe and protected eternally.

Jesus concludes these imperatives with a surprising explanation of this teaching. The reason to store treasure securely and eternally in heaven rather than vulnerably and temporarily on earth is not rooted in the intrinsic value of the treasure but in the predictable human tendency to follow our treasure with our hearts. Jesus recognizes that the human heart follows treasure. So, to put one's treasure in heaven means that one's heart will be drawn closer to God.

Several of the words and phrases used in this passage connect to other passages in Matthew. Jesus later describes to the rich young ruler that "treasure in heaven" is money given to the poor (Matthew 19:21). Similarly, Jesus has already blessed the pure in heart in Matthew 5:8. He has also condemned the adulterer in heart (Matthew 5:28). The word "heart" is used about 16 times in Matthew. Jesus says that major sins come from the heart (Matthew 15:8, 19–20).

He also says to forgive from the heart and love God with all of one's heart (Matthew 18:35, 22:37). The heart matters to Jesus. He calls His community to have hearts following after heaven by placing our treasure there.

The second major point contains no imperatives. It illustrates the devastating consequences of orienting your life towards materialism. Whether people store their treasure on earth or in heaven, their eyes inevitably look toward that treasure. The eye is like a lamp of the body that takes in whatever it sees. If your eyes look toward heaven, then your body is filled with the light of God. If your eyes look toward wealth and materialism, then your eyes will be clouded, and darkness will enter your body. That darkness can grow and spread, and the internal light will dim into utter darkness. This passage connects with Matthew's theme of contrasting light and darkness (Matthew 4:16, 5:14–16). Darkness is the fate of those excluded from the kingdom (Matthew 8:12, 22:13, 25:30). Darkness covered the earth at the crucifixion of Jesus (Matthew 27:45). Darkness is what Jesus came to overcome with His saving light (Matthew 4:16–17). And darkness is what enters and consumes the body through an eye fixed on wealth.

The third major point also contains no imperatives. It further illustrates the dreadful reality of serving wealth. If one stores up treasure on earth and fixes an eye on money, that person will inevitably serve money. One who serves money cannot also serve God. Jesus states that one cannot serve two masters without loving one and hating the other. Jesus does not teach a healthy balance. He does not teach that multiple masters are fine so long as God edges out the others. He believes in picking a side. He believes in ultimate, singular, unwavering loyalty to God.

The fourth major point gets back to using imperatives:

"Do not be worried about your life" (Matthew 6:25). "Look at the birds of the air" (Matthew 6:26). "Observe how the lilies of the field grow" (Matthew 6:28). "Seek first His kingdom and His righteousness" (Matthew 6:33). In this passage, Jesus repeatedly challenges His disciples not to worry (Matthew 6:25, 31, 34). He argues from the lesser to the greater based on observation in nature. God clothes the flowers and feeds the birds. Yet, He considers His human children to be of even greater value than plants and animals. We should be willing to trust Him to feed and clothe us. This is why Jesus tells His followers to pay attention to the flowers and birds. There are lessons to learn from how God runs His world. Worry does not feed birds or clothe flowers, and it will do nothing valuable for you. So, seek His kingdom and His righteousness. Trust in His care, and take delight in the blessings of today. Words like "kingdom" (Matthew 5:3, 10, 19, 20; 6:10, 33; 7:21) and "righteousness" (Matthew 5:6, 10, 20; 6:1, 33) are both central themes in this pericope and the entire Sermon on the Mount.

APPLICATION

Give Your Sole Allegiance to God: One thing that consistently runs throughout this passage is that God wants our sole allegiance. Wealth often competes with God for the human heart. We are not told to store treasure on earth and in heaven. We are not told to have one eye on God and one eye on our possessions. We are not told to serve God and wealth. We're told that is impossible. We are told to choose one or the other.

Give Up Hoarding: Jesus does not command us to starve or wander naked and homeless. In fact, He says that

God will provide what we need (Matthew 6:33), and that includes food, clothes, and shelter. Jesus does not condemn using or enjoying money. He condemns hoarding money. If Jesus is to be believed, amassing treasure creates a significant temptation that almost no one can overcome (Matthew 19:23–24).

Today Matters: One reason we are so tempted to hoard wealth is fear that we will lose it. Jesus admits clearly that treasure on earth does not last, can become useless, or can be stolen. If we hoard wealth because we are worried about tomorrow, then we need to take a look around at the flowers and birds and begin trusting God more. We need to be content and thankful for what we have today.

Trust God: Anxiety, while a universal experience that pops up from time to time, should not be the constant state in which we live. I offer no medical or psychiatric evaluations in this study. I'm not denying that anxiety can be helped with medical treatment and intervention. But if our anxiety is regularly associated with money, even when we have food, clothes, and a home, then it may indicate that our materialism has assaulted our trust in God. If we have God, we have more than we will ever need (Psalm 73:25–28, 1 Timothy 6:17–19).

CONCLUSION

This text is so valuable because I often fail to live up to it. It is one of those gnawing teachings that I'd much rather ignore, dilute, or exegete around. I'd love to say that Jesus is actually okay with storing treasure on earth, provided we also store treasure in heaven. However, I must face the fact that Jesus did not say that. He also did not tell us how much counts as "storing." He did not give a specific financial limit.

There probably is not one universal rule. This is also not the only teaching in the Bible on money. However, when I am thinking more about the stock market than the kingdom, I know I am heading in the wrong direction. When I let financial frustration cause me to be short with others, or when I dedicate time to brainstorming avenues for generating more income, but I haven't done the same for ways to love my neighbor or reach others with the gospel, then I know I'm off track. This passage helps keep me focused on what truly matters in life.

DISCUSSION QUESTIONS

1. What are some helpful warning signs that one has started storing up treasure on earth or serving wealth?
2. If there is any limit to how much earthly treasure a Christian should possess, what might it be?
3. What are some natural connections between wealth, trust, and anxiety?
4. How can observing nature help us understand God?
5. What are some ways you've seen God keep His word in Matthew 6:33?

RELEASE TO FORGIVE

GOD'S MODEL FOR FORGIVENESS APPLIED

JEFF JOHNSON

TEXT

> For if you forgive men their trespasses, your heavenly
> Father will also forgive you. But if you do not forgive men
> their trespasses, neither will your Father forgive your tres-
> passes (Matthew 6:14–15).

INTRODUCTION

Examining our text indicates a certain simplicity in the
command to forgive. We find "If / Then" logic. If we want
forgiveness, we must forgive. However, human behavior
complicates a seemingly simple principle. In addition, we
find instruction in God's word to separate ourselves from
unrepentant sinners (1 Corinthians 6:9–11, 2 Thessalonians 3:6). Theologians seem to swing from one end of the
radical spectrum to forgive in all cases to the inference of
grudge-holding against the unrepentant. Is there, in fact, a
contradiction, or is there a balance that requires deeper

consideration? We must ask ourselves, "How has God modeled and instructed us to forgive?" As we explore this idea, we may discover a need to refine our definition of the word "forgiveness." In addition, we will examine a few related words for clarity.

Defining Forgiveness

Baker's Bible Encyclopedia gives us an explanation of "forgiveness."

> Ceasing to feel resentment for wrongs and offenses; pardon, involving restoration of broken relationships. Primarily, forgiveness is an act of God, releasing sinners from judgment and freeing them from the divine penalty of their sin. Since only God is holy, only God can forgive sin (Mark 2:7, Luke 5:21). Forgiveness is also a human act toward one's neighbor, given new incentive and emphasis in the NT because of God's forgiveness in the death of Christ. Hence, forgiveness is a uniquely Christian doctrine.[1]

The Bible indicates that redemption is required for the forgiveness of man's sin. "In Him, we have redemption through His blood, the forgiveness of sins, according to the riches of His grace" (Ephesians 1:7).[2] This forgiveness of sin is God removing our transgression from memory (Hebrews 8:12). This redemption or forgiveness is found in obedience to the Gospel, which is defined in 1 Corinthians 15:1–4. As Christ died on the cross, dying to oneself is repentance (Acts 17:30) and confession (Matthew 10:32), which leads to a new identity, a transformation in death to oneself. The old creature is then buried in baptism, as

Christ was buried in the tomb. Being raised from the water, as Christ was resurrected, the new creature (2 Corinthians 5:17) walks in a new life (Romans 6:3–4). Notice that God has released forgiveness to all of humanity. However, one must be obedient to the gospel to receive it (2 Thessalonians 1:8). Forgiveness from God is well explained within His word. Still, some take pieces of His plan of salvation and add man-made ideas, marketing them falsely as God's saving grace. This is a failure to "diligently seek Him" (Hebrews 11:6).

There is likely a similar problem in our understanding of forgiveness, one toward another. Let us remember that God is forgiving, and yet, not all are forgiven. God is also just (Revelation 15:3). Justice demands consequences for behavior. Who, then, is in the position to exact justice? Paul tells us that we are to subject ourselves to civil authority (Romans 13:1–2). What if the civil authority fails?

When the personal human justice system is violated, we find ourselves angry. Anger is a God-given emotion that comes with instruction. Paul's inspired pen tells us to "be angry and sin not" (Ephesians 4:26). Unresolved anger leads to wrath and grudges, which are self-destructive activities that God has warned us against (Leviticus 19:18). God is plain that vengeance belongs to Him (Romans 12:19, Hebrews 10:30–31).

Now, we find a human dilemma. What do we do when our personal justice system is violated? What do we do with wrath, grudges, and the desire for revenge? Perhaps looking at three case studies held up to the light of God's word will help us see what our responses should look like.

CASE STUDIES

The content of these case studies contains material that some readers may find disturbing—including references to suicide, sexual violence, drunk driving, and parental abuse.

Unfair

Imagine a wife coming home after a full day's work at the office to find her children murdered and her husband having committed suicide. Kimberly's mind wandered back to a noontime call from her husband inviting her home for lunch. It is likely he planned to eradicate the entire family. Some would say she must forgive him lest she rot in resentment. May she do that if he is not alive to seek and receive forgiveness? This murder/suicide is a true story detailed in a book titled *Unfair*.[3] Kimberly walks the reader through her range of emotions with the helpful guide of her therapist, Dr. Terry Gunnells.

Forgiveness, as we see from Biblical models, requires the interaction of at least two. Jesus instructs us to first go to the individual who offended us (Matthew 18:15). What do WE do when that person is not there? We cannot logically offer forgiveness to someone who cannot repent of wrong and accept it. How can we forgive if we can no longer restore a relationship? One problem is that we automatically assume that unforgiveness equates with grudge-bearing. We know that bearing a grudge is not only sinful in God's sight, but we can see resentment as it grows and destroys. What do we do with these unresolved feelings when forgiveness is not possible?

Would it be fair to say we can release the offender to forgive? Essentially, we release anger and resentment to

God and submit ourselves to His justice. Jesus tells us, "But I say to you who hear: Love your enemies, do good to those who hate you, bless those who curse you, and pray for those who spitefully use you" (Luke 6:27–28).

Moses's anger with Aaron and the children of Israel resulted in his smashing the stone tablets on which the finger of God wrote the Ten Commandments. Exodus 34 tells us of the incident that replaced the tablets, including an applicable description of God.

> Now the LORD descended in the cloud and stood with him there, and proclaimed the name of the LORD. And the LORD passed before him and proclaimed, "The LORD, the LORD God, merciful and gracious, longsuffering, and abounding in goodness and truth, keeping mercy for thousands, forgiving iniquity and transgression and sin, by no means clearing the guilty, visiting the iniquity of the fathers upon the children and the children's children to the third and the fourth generation" (Exodus 34:5–7).

God presents Himself with mercy and a willingness to forgive. Yet, some abuse their God-given right to choose and find themselves righteously unforgiven. Certainly, sinful actions impact others. However, we can take comfort in that God will serve justice as He sees fit in His time. We do not have to go on record saying we have forgiven, but that we have released the situation into God's hands and, therefore, have peace.

The Drunk Driver

The grandfather of a young Christian woman was killed

in the middle of the day by a drunk driver in a head-on collision. The driver had avoided previous convictions concerning inebriated driving with outstanding legal counsel. The simple situation is that the justice system failed in this case, and a repeat offender committed manslaughter.

In court, the offender had a statement read where he apologized for the incident and begged for mercy from the family and the judge. The offender's face appeared less than remorseful. How would you feel as a young Christian woman?

She wandered through feelings of anger at the justice system and the offender. It was obvious that the offender's apology had the air of "I am sorry I got caught." The lack of sincerity and remorse for the impact of his actions increased her anger. What does she do with that anger?

Again, as Luke recorded in chapter six, we pray. We pray for those we perceive as enemies and ask God to give us wisdom and peace. We release to God the unmanageable. We should be mindful that our challenges may refine or harden us. Choosing James's guidance will provide us with comfort and peace.

> My brethren, count it all joy when you fall into various trials, knowing that the testing of your faith produces patience. But let patience have its perfect work, that you may be perfect and complete, lacking nothing. If any of you lacks wisdom, let him ask of God, who gives to all liberally and without reproach, and it will be given to him (James 1:2–5).

In every life challenge, one should ask, "What is God trying to teach me now?" In our moments of refinement, looking for lessons and points we can use to help others is the superior choice.

The Abusive Father

A young girl at the age of ten was suffering from the trauma of parental malfunction. The parents were Christians in appearance. Her father had developed alcoholism, and her mother had become an enabler. As his condition worsened, his traffic violations resulted in the loss of his license. However, his reasoning became impaired, and he felt entitled to drive to work. In addition, he had drunken fits of rage that could be heard down the street. Friends and neighbors saw all this, and the wife explained everything away, at least she thinks.

One evening, in a mindless drunken stupor, he got up and went to his daughter's room and committed the unspeakable with his ten-year-old daughter. This incident began a horrific story of two years of torture in repeated incidents. Many times, the daughter tried to tell her mother of the nightmare she was living, only to be accused of being a liar.

Then, one morning, in the early hours before daylight, the now twelve-year-old was subjected to another attack, but this time it was different. She managed to escape to a neighbor's house with her drunken father in pursuit. Neither was dressed as they scuffled on the neighbor's porch. The authorities were called, and the father was arrested.

When the father returned to a sober state and realized his location, he had a fit of rage. "Unlawful detainment!" was his cry. This man's mind had become so numbed that he did not remember and denied what happened, even though there were many witnesses.

What is this girl supposed to do with those confused feelings? She loves her father, but at the same time, she is enraged at his behavior. She also loves her mother, who has done nothing to protect her for two years.

Her mother begs forgiveness. Our text is clear that the forgiveness sought is to be granted. But what about her father, who denies the abuse? Matthew brings his account of the words of Jesus concerning our enemies in chapter five, verse forty-four. "But I say to you, love your enemies, bless those who curse you, do good to those who hate you, and pray for those who spitefully use you and persecute you."

Prayer is the answer to the human dilemma. Whether a person asks forgiveness or not, the wise child of God approaches His throne with their pain.

CONCLUSION

Our text and study make it abundantly clear that the child of God must always be willing to forgive. Exploring Paul's inspired pen in this regard may give us a stronghold. "And now abide faith, hope, love, these three; but the greatest of these is love" (1 Corinthians 13:13).

First, we must trust God and have faith that His direction is always best. A physician may prescribe a medicine that tastes bitter yet provides healing. In like manner, Jesus has given us a prescription for healing relationships that have been damaged.

> Moreover, if your brother sins against you, go and tell him his fault between you and him alone. If he hears you, you

have gained your brother. But if he will not hear, take with you one or two more, that by the mouth of two or three witnesses every word may be established. And if he refuses to hear them, tell it to the church. But if he refuses even to hear the church, let him be to you like a heathen and a tax collector (Matthew 18:15–17).

In this case, we see that one may be righteously unforgiven. We do not find instruction to continue to harbor anger and resentment, but to cut off fellowship.

Second, Paul mentions "hope." In this study, we can see that a willingness to forgive would employ hope for another. Praying for a peaceful restoration of the relationship is certainly in order. However, we must not dwell on those who continue in evil, lest we, too, be entangled.

Finally, Paul wraps back to love as inspirationally defined. Love seeks the best for others. God has modeled His infinite love for us so we may learn to exhibit the same. After all, our duty is to fear God and keep His commands (Ecclesiastes 13:13). We allow Him to be seen in us when we exhibit His love.

DISCUSSION QUESTIONS

1. God's model of forgiveness shows us that an incident is forgotten. What does that look like?
2. Explain the difference between forgiveness and releasing an unmanageable situation to God.
3. How often should God be involved in the conflict of human affairs, and how?
4. Is it possible to be righteously unforgiven? Describe such a situation.

5. What would phrases sound like in a prayer offered from an injured heart?
6. May an unfaithful spouse be forgiven? May an unfaithful spouse be righteously unforgiven and released?
7. If a brother/sister were caught stealing from the church treasury, are we obligated to forgive if asked? Would it be wise to give this person the same access as before?
8. If a brother/sister were convicted of any crime, are we obligated to forgive if asked?
9. Is it wise to take preventative action in the case of a forgiven individual?
10. Should we approach a brother/sister who has been convicted of a crime in an effort to restore such a one?

ENDNOTES

[1] James M. Houston, "Forgiveness," in *Baker Encyclopedia of the Bible* (Grand Rapids, MI: Baker Book House, 1988), 810.

[2] *The New King James Version* (Nashville, TN: Thomas Nelson, 1982), Eph 1:7.

[3] Kimberly Griffith and Terry Gunnells, *Unfair* (Montgomery, AL: Emma Jay Publishing, 1997).

JUDGE NOT

MATTHEW 7:1–5

JORDAN GRAY

Judge not, that you be not judged.
　　Matthew 7:1

A POLARIZING PASSAGE

Matthew 7:1–5 occupies a special place among Scripture's most polarizing passages, wedged somewhere between those who ironically quote the Bible in an effort to deny Biblical authority, and those who are so intoxicated with Biblical authority that they usurp it. The first crowd shouts, "You can't judge us! Just read Matthew 7!" The second retorts, "Yes, we can! Read it again!" As Christians and non-Christians alike recruit this passage to suit their own needs, let us humble ourselves before the Lord of the passage, asking afresh what He said and what He intends us to do with it as disciples.

In particular, let us consider why our Lord summed up His admonition in the two words, "Judge not." Many have expounded upon the balance of the passage, interpreting Jesus's overall message as "Judge rightly," and for good reason. Even within the Sermon, it is obvious that Christians must judge in some sense of the word; else how could they beware of false prophets (7:15)? When Jesus said, "You will recognize them by their fruits" (7:20), He said in effect, "You will judge."

And yet, Jesus chose in this instance not to say, "Judge rightly," but to say, "Judge not." Leaving aside all that could be said of the balanced, whole counsel of Christ on this topic of judging, let us focus here specifically on the danger towards which Jesus has weighted His words. Instead of averaging out the Scriptures and establishing what right we do have to judge, let us hear the warning of Christ and consider why it is that He commands, "Judge not."

ONE LAWGIVER. ONE JUDGE.

In an epistle that is deeply colored by his brother's Sermon, James speaks against those who would take up the role of judge rather than "doer of the law." He demands, "There is only one lawgiver and judge, he who is able to save and destroy. But who are you to judge your neighbor" (James 4:12)? At issue for James is not whether a given judgment is fair or accurate. James simply asks who we think we are, presuming to sit in the judgment seat of God.

Jesus warns us to judge not, firstly because we forget our rightful place as those who stand under God's judgment. He says, "Judge not, *that you be not judged*"—be mindful of your own judgment. Craig Keener suggests, "By this point in the Sermon, no one who has been taking Jesus's words seriously will feel much like judging anyone else anyway."[1] Jesus knows that those who are genuinely mindful of their own sins and who are grateful for the undeserved mercies of God will also be those who have the least interest for judging others.

On the other hand, Jesus knows the grotesque disfigurement of a prideful heart usurping the throne of God. Jesus tells stories such as the two who went up to the temple to pray (Luke 18:9–14) and the unforgiving servant (Matthew 18:23–35), highlighting the ways we misjudge and abuse others when we first misjudge our own standing before God. We become like Jonah, opposing God's grace toward others because we have not internalized God's grace toward ourselves, nor have we understood our need of it.

And so, Jesus suggests that our first judgments be for ourselves: "First take the log out of your own eye." The sins we are most able to judge (and those which should be most personally concerning) are our own. If we are to judge rightly at all, it will only be after we have dealt with God for our own sakes, not only because we will then proceed with clear reason, but most importantly because we will proceed with a loving and grateful heart, washed in the grace of salvation. Again, from James, "So speak and so act as those who are to be judged under the law of liberty. For judgment is without mercy to one who has shown no mercy. Mercy triumphs over judgment" (James 2:12–13).

WHY DO YOU SEE THE SPECK?

A second reason for Jesus's warning against judgment is because we tend to do it so poorly. Notice this basic assumption in Jesus's line of questioning, where He addresses His hearers as though they tend to be hypocrites in this regard. Why do you all judge like hypocrites? The fact is that judgment is a serious matter, and God is very slow to entrust it to a people who do it so poorly.

In Jesus's parable of the weeds (Matthew 13:24–30), the master refused his servants' offer to gather the weeds out of his wheat field, reasoning, "lest in gathering the weeds you root up the wheat along with them" (13:29). In rooting up weeds, we often cause unintended collateral damage, hurting the kingdom by our carelessness or thoughtlessness. God is the only one who separates sheep from goats perfectly. And, many times, we are mistaken in our assessment of who is weed and who is wheat. Darnel (the particular weed of Jesus's parable) looks very similar to wheat, and the master is rightly concerned that his untrained and overzealous servants might confuse the two. And, since he cannot trust them to execute judgment, he instructs, "Let both grow together until the harvest" (13:30). Jesus would have us forgo judgment rather than damage the kingdom with poor judgment.

We judge poorly because we are personally invested in the rationalization and defense of our own sins, whereas the sins of others actually work to prove our comparative goodness. We up-play the sins of others, and we down-play our own. Joe Bayly tells of a former Nazi he met who had participated in the Holocaust. Interestingly, the man complained that he had once missed a promotion because he objected to social dancing.[2] What is it in the soul of a man that can simultaneously rationalize violent cruelty while condemning dancing? And, lest we take satisfaction in judging the soldier, may we recognize that we also carry this inconsistency in our souls as a universal trait of broken humanity. We're not good judges.

Jesus would have us address the personal failings that make us such poor judges, removing logs before picking at specks. And yet, we must acknowledge the fact that only Jesus has perfectly clear sight. Even at our best, undiscovered or intransigent specks cloud our vision, and we can never proceed to judgment apart from the sobering awareness of our limitations as flawed human beings.

Then You Will See Clearly

We have focused on the dangers of judging, which give us pause, but let us think about what it means to love our brothers through accountability before we close. While we acknowledge God as the one judge over all, and we confess our failings as poor judges, we also see that true love does not sit back and watch as sin destroys. When we love others, we desire that they break free from sin and experience the joy of Christ. How should we then address our brother in his sin?

Firstly, it needs to be said that we should address him! How often do we judge the sins of our brother from a distance, never meeting him face to face? John Wesley wondered,

> But how rarely should we condemn or judge one another ... were we to walk by that clear and express rule which our Lord himself has taught us! "If thy brother shall trespass against thee ... go and tell him of his fault, between him and thee alone."[3]

Yet, we do not meet our brother face to face because we know what a messy business it will be. We will have to contend with his thoughts, not just our own. We will have to deal with details and extenuating circumstances that we do not yet know. We will no longer get by with the cold, hard rationality of our detached imagination, but we will have to engage with the unpredictable and uncontrollable—

emotions, variables, paradoxes. In short, we prefer to judge from a distance because personal connection changes everything. But that is the way of love. Do we truly love?

And secondly, we must engage our brother through sympathetic identification. The apostle Paul became all things to all people because of his love for them, and it is no stretch at all to identify with fellow sinners as such.

When approaching a brother in his sin, Augustine wrote of the levels of identification he worked through. He said,

> We must first reflect whether the fault is one that we have never had or one from which we are now free. If we have never had it, let us reflect that we are only human and might have had it. If we have had it and no longer have it, let it be impressed upon the memory that here is a weakness shared by us, so that not hatred but pity will go out in advance of our chiding or upbraiding. If on reflection we find ourselves involved in the same fault as he whom we are preparing to chide, let us not chide nor rebuke; but let us sorrow from our heart; let us invite him not to conform himself to us, but to join us in a common resolve.[4]

When we truly see all of our relationships in the light of our ultimate relationship to God as King and Savior, we will not posture nor pretend, but we will know of a certainty that we share an identity with every lost sinner and that through Jesus Christ we have been saved by grace. Let us then worship Him as the only lawgiver and judge, gratefully receiving the joy of salvation in Him and drawing others to receive it for themselves, as well.

DISCUSSION QUESTIONS

1. In what ways am I pressed by my culture (church, family, community, etc.) to apply this passage? Do I have any bias to be judgmental? Do I have any bias to resist judgment?
2. Am I bothered more by the sins of others (in my family, community, world) or by my own sins?
3. Describe a time when someone else judged you unfairly. What was it that made them poorly qualified to be your judge? Have you ever exhibited any of those same traits in your judgment of others?
4. Think through Augustine's framework for identifying with others in sin. Is it hard for you to identify with other sinners and approach them in this way? Why or why not?

ENDNOTES

[1] Craig S. Keener, *Matthew* (The IVP New Testament Commentary Series; Downers Grove, IL: InterVarsity Press, 1997), 156.

[2] Keener, *Matthew,* 158.

[3] Kenneth J. Collins and Jason E. Vickers, eds., *The Sermons of John Wesley: A Collection for the Christian Journey* (Nashville, TN: Abingdon, 2013), 376.

[4] Johannes Quasten and Joseph C. Plumpe, eds., *St. Augustine: The Lord's Sermon on the Mount,* trans. John J. Jepson, ACW 5 (Mahwah, NJ: Paulist, 1948), 152.

BIBLIOGRAPHY

Collins, Kenneth J., and Jason E. Vickers, eds. *The Sermons of John Wesley: A Collection for the Christian Journey.* Nashville, TN: Abingdon, 2013.

Keener, Craig S. *Matthew.* The IVP New Testament Commentary Series. Downers Grove, IL: InterVarsity Press, 1997.

Quasten, Johannes, and Joseph C. Plumpe, eds. *St. Augustine: The Lord's Sermon on the Mount.* Translated by John J. Jepson. ACW 5. Mahwah, NJ: Paulist, 1948.

Matthew 7:6–26

Baron Vander Maas

The Main Idea

Jesus gives the hearers two choices at the conclusion of His sermon. You can choose holiness, righteousness, and life, or you can choose complacency, sin, and death. The same choice falls into our laps today as well.

Introduction

Thirty-one flavors is quite a lot! In fact, that is the selling point for the ice cream franchise, Baskin-Robbins. If you want ice cream, you ought to go to the place where you have an abundance of choices. But how can you try them all? Well, that's also a selling point. Because you cannot try them all in one visit, you return to try the flavors you didn't get to taste. The choices are seemingly endless! In American culture, an abundance of choices is the norm. With food, especially, many different restaurants give multi-page menus with many appetizers, entrees, and desserts. Or even think about the worldwide network of Amazon, Etsy, eBay, and Walmart, which gives the ability to buy anything you could possibly want at a moment's notice. We are given choices constantly in a consumerist society; a society that seeks every way to get our money. With all of our choices, we can be fooled into believing that choices are ever abundant and the right choice is whatever makes us feel good. That is not the case as it relates to Christ. When we turn to Matthew 7, we find that there are two choices in front of us: life and death.

Digging Deeper

In Matthew 7:6–12, as Jesus wraps up His sermon, He offers a reminder to consider those who will hear and receive the gospel. Using the images of dogs and pigs, Jesus warns not to give what is holy out to disgusting creatures that trample on the purity or the uniqueness of the gift (envisioned as a pearl). The precious gift of the gospel, when shared with those who do not want it, reviles and ridicules the message. This does not mean that we avoid sharing the gospel, but instead, if someone does not want to hear it, we shake the dust off our feet and go to the next house (Matthew 10:13–14).[1]

Jesus moves to the relationship between the Father and His people.

> Ask, and it will be given to you; seek, and you will find; knock, and it will be opened to you. For everyone who asks receives, and the one who seeks finds, and to the one who knocks it will be opened (Matthew 7:7–8 ESV).

Prayer and supplication to God are Christian practices that ought to be exercised daily. The same favor God gives to you is what He expects you to give to your neighbor. "Whatever you wish that others would do to you, do also to them ..." (Matthew 7:12). Jesus wants us to treat others with the same compassion and kindness that we expect for ourselves. Linking concepts from verses 7–12 that the reciprocal relationship between God's servant and God is what they ought to expect from one another. God is generous and kind; ask and He will surely give to you. God's servants follow God's example in showing generosity to God, but also generosity to others. To follow Christ is to learn kindness and then provide it faithfully to everyone in their path, because that is how you would want to be treated (v. 12).

At the end of the Sermon on the Mount, Jesus gives an invitation to make a choice. Unlike Baskin-Robbins, there are only two choices. Will you take the broad way or the narrow way? Jesus defines the results (life and death), but He also prepares hearers for the difficulty of each (easy and hard).[2] The metaphor of a path illustrates to the readers that the destination you ultimately desire is determined by whether you are willing to live in difficulty now or instead pursue an easy existence. This reminds me of the common expression, "The way to hell feels like heaven, but the way to heaven feels like hell."

You can choose to be one of two trees: a healthy tree bearing fruit or a diseased tree bearing nothing. Jesus tells us that we are recognized by our fruits (Matthew 7:20), which means the fruit produced is obvious and impactful for those around us (cf. Galatians 5:16–24). A tree that is healthy illustrates a Christian who is devoted and faithful, living out his or her convictions (cf. Matthew 21:18–22). A tree that is diseased or dead is not good for anything. The fruit, the roots, the branches, and the leaves are all bad;

therefore, it might as well be thrown in the fire, a reference to eternal judgment (Matthew 7:19).

Lastly, there are going to be two types of people who proclaim "Lord, Lord:" true disciples and false disciples. The balance of activity and faithfulness is clear in this section. A servant is to be active in his life for the kingdom of God, but activity alone is not salvation. There will be those who do the right things, say the right words, and act in the right manner, but never truly know Jesus. Why did they not know Jesus? Because they did not do those things in the name of the Father (Matthew 7:21). How sad it would be to know all of the right answers but still not pass on the final day.

APPLICATION

Have you ever tried to figure out where to eat dinner with your family? The talk begins, "Where do you want to eat?" The response is normally, "It doesn't matter to me!" However, though it does not matter, you still can't agree on a location. It is a painful process trying to satisfy both parties. One reason is that there are too many choices. Mexican, Chinese, burgers, steaks, seafood, or home country cooking are just a small list of all the options you may have in your local town. Being stuck with a ton of choices often makes it harder to choose. The "paradox of choice" is that people get so consumed with choices that they end up not making any at all! This definitely happens in the Christian world. What church should I attend? What books should I read? What doctrine am I supposed to read? These questions become barriers to action. I am not suggesting that Christians should refrain from asking these questions in regular practice. However, too many choices can lead to too much analysis, which can lead to stagnation in the Christian life. We are so busy wondering what to do that we do nothing at all.

People believe that the Christian life is millions of choices you have to make in your whole life. And maybe that is true to an extent. But let us start with one decision: Will you follow Jesus or follow Satan? The Sermon on the Mount is a life-changing exhortation about true personal development. The Christian life starts from the heart and leads to the hands and feet. Seek first the Kingdom of God and his righteousness (Matthew 6:33). Seeking God's rule is to seek a righteousness outside of ourselves, contrary to the Pharisees (Matthew 5:17–20). The choice to follow Jesus is to choose His way of life, follow in His footsteps, and accept His authority. The difficulty of that choice is that it leads, like Jesus, for others to persecute and revile us (Matthew 5:11–12). But great is the reward in heaven for those who valiantly and faithfully commit to Christ. Following Jesus is to make the choice to seek after life and godliness.

Refusing to follow Jesus becomes the inevitable choice to follow Satan. Satan's way is a self-satisfying endeavor. The individual wants an easy life with no heartache, pain, or difficulty. Not only is it the avoidance of difficulty, but the ultimate striving for pleasure. Many want an easy life, and many will find it. Whether it be wealth, food, or fame, many are searching for "life" outside of Christ, and they will never find anything as fulfilling as Him. Many may find pleasure, but it turns out it will be evident they are a diseased tree. Who is the one who brings more peace, righteousness, and goodness to the world around them? Or are we going to be hedonists who satisfy our own appetites rather than satisfy the will of God? This is the easiest choice with the most downfall.

What is an even worse danger than just being a pleasure seeker in the way of Satan, is to seek pleasure but believe you are seeking Jesus. Many will approach Jesus and shout, "Lord, Lord!" But the truth is, there are some who do the right things, say the right stuff, and their hearts are far from Him. To be a faithful Christian, our hearts beg for Jesus daily, they desire His will, and they meet with Him always. We only have one choice in this life; will you choose today to follow Christ?

DISCUSSION QUESTIONS

1. Read Matthew 7:6–23. If you were to give one word to describe all of these passages together, what word would it be and why?
2. Jesus says the "narrow way" is the more difficult way that leads to life. Why do you think difficulty produces a better outcome? Where in the Sermon on the Mount do we see this same concept of difficulty being worth the effort?

ENDNOTES

[1] Donald A. Hagner, *Matthew 1–13*, Word Biblical Commentary 33A (Nashville: Thomas Nelson, 1993), 172.

[2] For more information on the two paths, see Ed Gallagher, *The Sermon on the Mount: Explorations in Christian Practice* (Florence: Heritage University Press, 2021), 207–219.

WISE AND FOOLISH LISTENERS

MATTHEW 7:24–29

GEORGE HULETT

FOCUS PASSAGE

Matthew 7:24–29

ONE MAIN THOUGHT

There's a big difference between hearing and listening.

INTRODUCTION

"Four score and seven years ago, our forefathers ..." You know the rest. "I have a dream that my four little children will one day live in a nation where they will not be judged by the color of their skin but by the content of their character ..." "Ask not what your country can do for you ..." There are some speeches that are memorable and some that are probably less so. What makes the difference? Is it the spellbinding ability of the speaker, or the depth of the discussion, or possibly even the passion behind the presentation? It's probably a little bit of all of these combined, but more than these are the words themselves. Whether simple everyday words or $5 fancy expressions, the words are what make the speech memorable. And so it is with Jesus's great Sermon on the Mount. It's only about a hundred verses containing about 2300 words or so. (That's about a 25–30 minute Sunday morning sermon.) So why is it so memorable? Because the words He used were life-changing.

He called for people to take the laws and commands of God to heart and not just at face value. It's not enough to just avoid stealing and adultery and murder. He pointed at the heart and said, Don't even dwell on these things. And thus, in just a short sermon, He touched on the very essence of righteousness before God. That's why this sermon has stood the test of time.

As He concluded His remarks, He used a parable about wise and foolish builders to challenge them to implement His teachings and not just to hear the words.

GOING DEEPER

Jesus divides His hearers into two groups. Some would hear and do what He said, and others would not. His point is that it's easy to listen without commitment, but that real commitment requires dedication and, oftentimes, change.

"Whoever hears these sayings of Mine, and does them …" Several times a day, a train goes by my office. Trains are loud, and they whistle at three intersections within a few hundred feet of our building. But I rarely pay them any attention whatsoever. I hear them, but I'm not listening. There was a large crowd present when Jesus preached this lesson. Surely everybody could hear Him, but there is a big difference between hearing and listening. Often, we hear what we want to hear, as we listen with preset filters. Other times, we hear, but we don't respond. Jesus is saying that if we hear what He says and do what He asks, happiness is a serendipity of a right relationship with God. In fact, Luke records Jesus as saying, "More than that, blessed are those who hear the word of God and keep it!" (Luke 11:28) And isn't it true that those who can put aside anger and lust and greed are happier and live more fulfilling lives? A truly wise person will listen and heed the words of our Lord.

"A wise man who built on a rock ..." Years ago, I went to inspect a house that had been built down in south Arkansas. The homeowner had removed a large tree in order to place his house just right for a great view. He filled in the hole, and the contractor started building with the corner of the house in the middle of the fill. When I inspected the house after completion, I noted that one corner literally moved when you walked on it. South Arkansas is swampy, and a big hole filled with dirt quickly becomes just another mud pit. There was nothing to support the corner, and it bounced up and down with very little effort. If we're going to build a house, we want a firm foundation. And if we are going to build our lives, it had better be upon a firm foundation as well. Peter said, "Lord, to whom shall we go? You have the words of eternal life" (John 6:88). And Paul is very clear about the importance of our foundation: "For no one can lay any foundation other than the one already laid, which is Jesus Christ" (1 Corinthians 3:11).

"The rain descended, the floods came, and the winds blew and beat on that house; and it did not fall ..." Rain is coming. Storms are as sure as day and night. Some will be strong. They will shake your very foundations. There will be pain and disappointment and discouragement. Sometimes, you will feel the weight of the whole world on your shoulders. And in those times, you'd better have a secure foundation. But we don't have to be alone in those storms. We don't have to depend upon our own strength. Paul writes to Timothy to command the brethren to do good works, for "In this way they will lay up treasure for themselves as a firm foundation for the coming age, so that they may take hold of the life that is truly life" (1 Timothy 6:19).

"But everyone who hears these sayings of Mine, and does not do them ..." Sadly, there were some listening to Jesus that day who had no intention of following Him. Whether they were predetermined not to believe as the Pharisees and Sadducees were, or whether they were just there out of curiosity, or whether they had hard hearts and closed their ears, many did not immediately turn from their ways and start following God from the depths of their hearts. Sadly, there are many today who can read the words and continue on with their lives as if the words mean nothing at all. One example that we often encounter in ministry is the phrase, "I know what it says. But God would want me to be happy." That's not what Jesus said here. God wants us to be obedient. Probably the most quoted verse in scripture is John 3:16. And there is no doubt about God's love for us. But the writer of Hebrews points out that saving faith involves diligently seeking God (Hebrews 11:6) and then follows with many examples of faith being evidenced by works of obedience.

"The people were astonished at His teaching ..." When we share God's word, we use book, chapter, and verse; and thus we should. We are not teaching on our own authority. In fact, for this lesson, we are using Matthew's writings. But when Jesus spoke, people were amazed because He didn't need to quote Matthew, Mark, or Paul. His words carried great weight because they recognized authority when He spoke. To them, it was as if Jesus was claiming to be The Authority. And He was.

Years ago, there was a series of commercials on TV that used the slogan, "When E.F. Hutton talks, people listen." They'd always feature people going about their lives, but coming to a sudden stop to hear whatever was being said. I guess it was effective, as I still remember them. When Jesus spoke, people stopped what they were doing to listen. And they still do. It's not just the hearing, but what they do with His words makes all the difference. We can build on the rigid rock, or we can build on the shifting sand. It's our choice.

DISCUSSION QUESTIONS

1. In what areas of our lives do we find it much easier to hear the words of Jesus than to do them?

2. Specifically in this sermon, Jesus addressed: loving our enemies, forgiveness, humility, anger, lust, prayer, giving, divorce, and hypocrisy. Is this where we turn when questions about any of these issues arise? If not, why not?

3. Can we truly say we are building our house on a solid foundation if we follow only some of His words?

4. If our house were built partially on solid bedrock and partially in sandy soil, would it stand the test of time?

5. Why did Jesus's teachings seem to be so authoritative?

6. What one area of Jesus's teaching do we seem to
    neglect in our studies?

Scripture Index

CREDITS

Contributors

Travis Bookout (M.Div., Amridge University) is the Preaching Minister at Maryville Church of Christ in Maryville, Tennessee.

Michael Farris (BA 2010) is the Pulpit Minister for Oak Hill Church of Christ in Rome, Georgia. oak-hill.org.

Jordan Gray (MMin 2016) preaches for the Central congregation in Fayette, Alabama (facebook.com/central-cofcfayette). He and his wife, Priscilla, also work with couples and speak with churches concerning marriage crisis, glorifying God for the story of redemption He worked out in their own marriage.

George Hulett (BA 1998) has preached for the Downtown Church of Christ in Morrilton, Arkansas, since 2011.

Jeff Johnson (MMin 2024, Pursuing M.Div.) serves as the Pulpit Minister for the North Highlands Church of Christ in Russellville, Alabama.

Joshua Pappas (MMin 2019) serves as the Preaching Minister for LaVergne Church of Christ in LaVergne, TN. He is a graduate of Heritage Christian University with a

B.A. and M.Min. degrees. He has been married to his high school sweetheart, Keshia, for 28 years. He is one of the hosts of the Conversion Conversation Podcast. Contact him at pappy1975@gmail.com.

Frank C. Schipani (MMin 2018, Pursuing M.Div.) works for the Michigan Department of Corrections as a Probation Officer and volunteers as a MDOC Employee Wellness Chaplain. He also loves to teach the Word of God as the Chairman of Great Lakes Bible Bowl. He has served in youth and children's ministry in the past.

Don Snodgrass (MMin 2016) serves as a shepherd for the Sherrod Avenue church of Christ in Florence, Alabama. He is retired and involved with mission efforts, including teaching in the Philippines and South Africa.

Baron Vander Maas (MA Harding School of Theology) is the Minister at Mt. Zion Church of Christ, Florence, Alabama.

Cory Waddell (MDiv 2023) is the Pulpit Minister at Bear Valley Church of Christ, Denver, Colorado.

Eric R. Waller holds a PhD in Bible Exposition (Liberty University), a J. D. (Birmingham School of Law), Master's degrees (Harding School of Theology, and Fuller Theological Seminary), and a B.A. (Heritage Christian University). He has served as an adjunct professor at several seminaries, is the author of *A Biblical Theology of Water,* and makes his home in Pensacola, Florida.

Russell Wyatt (MMin 2017) is the Involvement Minister for the Church Street Church of Christ in Lewisburg, Tennessee.

Onesimus Bible Study Series

The Onesimus Bible Study Series offers biblical lessons for personal or group study from alumni of International Bible College/Heritage Christian University. Each lesson flows from confidence in Scripture as God's inspired, living, and powerful word. Each respects the ongoing relevance of the Bible as it shows us God's heart and guides our service in the name of Jesus. Every lesson is designed to build faith and encourage Christian living.

Love of the Faith: Favorite New Testament Texts (2023)

Refreshing the Saints: Favorite Old Testament Texts (2024)

Confident of Your Obedience: Favorite Sermon on the Mount Passages (2025)

Also by Cypress Publications

Berean Study Series

The Bond of Peace: The Seven Ones from Ephesians 4 (coming 2026)

God Battling for the Hearts of His People (2025)

Encountering the Gospel (2024)

Led by God's Spirit: A Practical Study of Galatians 5:22–26 (2023)

Majesty and Mercy: God Through the Eyes of Isaiah (2022)

For the Glory of God: Christ and the Church in Ephesians (2021)

Cloud of Witnesses: Ancient Stories of Faith (2020)

Visions of Grace (2019)

Instructions for Living: The Ten Commandments (2018)

Clothed in Christ: A How-to Guide (2017)

What Does Real Christianity Look Like? A Study of the Parables (2016)

The Ekklesia of Christ: Becoming the People of God (2015)

Radiant Study Series

CYPRESS

To see the full catalog of Heritage Christian University
Press and its imprint, Cypress Publications, visit
www.hcu.edu/publications